gratefully and affectionately
dedicated to the memory of
my former provincial superiors

Rev. Fr Emmanuel Crowther, s.j.
and
Rev. Fr William Moran, s.j.

who
encouraged and even enthused me in the
Apostolate of the Written and Spoken Word
and stood by me amidst incomprehension and
opposition
and
to whom
I owe, next to God,
the evangelical freedom I strove to exercise
in the field of theology.

GRATEFUL ACKNOWLEDGEMENT

The author and the Tulana community thank
Prof. Lieve Troch of the University of Neijmegen
for bearing the cost
of the publication of this book.

Thanks are due also to **Prof. Shirley Wijesinghe**
for helping the author with transliteration of Hebrew terms
and to **Mr. Leon Perumal** for drawing the charts.

ABREVIATIONS

EAPR : *East Asian Pastoral Review* (Manila)

VJTR : *Vidyajyoti Journal of Theological Reflection* (Delhi)

ATL : *Asian Theology of Liberation,* Orbis Books, Maryknoll, (NY) 1988

CONTENTS

INTRODUCTION
A Few Things to Remember
When Reading This Book

A theology that is relevant and contemporary

Some think — and would want others to think — that "Liberation theology" is out of fashion if not out of date altogether for the simple reason that it is not mentioned today as frequently as it used to be a few decades ago. This inference is flawed. That Liberation Theology has lost its novelty does not imply that it has lost its relevance. It is far from being extinct. For its framework can be detected even in certain tracts published by the Federation of Asian Bishops' Conferences (FABC)! Some evangelicals in our country are also showing overt interest in it. In fact I am grateful to the Colombo Theological College, the training centre for pastors mostly of the evangelical alliance, for inviting me to conduct a seminar on the biblical basis of an Asian Liberation Theology. It is reported that some Pentecostals in Latin America are having second thoughts about their early hostility towards it. In fact Liberation Theology is not restricted to poor countries; there is, for instance, a series of books published under the title *British Liberation Theology* edited by C. Rowland & J. Vincent in UK. Hence the present work on the genesis and the methodology of an *Asian Liberation Theology* is saturated with contemporary relevance for Asia and beyond!

"Asian" does *not* mean "Anti-Western"

The fact that an "Asian" Theology is not Western does not imply that it is necessarily Eastern because in

1

ecclesiastical parlance 'eastern' has become a blanket term for not only for oriental rite churches, which are Asian, but also for Greek traditions. There can be a confusion here. Greek culture and philosophies, though misnamed 'Eastern' by church historians, are the foundation of Western Christian thought, as Cardinal Ratzinger had insisted. If that is so, the word "Asian" can be applied only to the *non-Greek* "Eastern Rite churches" which even today employ a Semitic or Indic language in their liturgies. All the so-called "Eastern" churches other than those derived from the Greek Orthodox stream are, therefore, regarded as "Asian". For they have absorbed cultural characteristics of Asia. Their theologies and spirituality are truly Asian though some of them have been repudiated by Ecumenical Councils, which, let us remember, defined doctrines in the language and the philosophy of the Greeks .

Note that the Arian or Aryan languages that migrated to Asia, such as those derived from Vedic and Sanskrit, even though categorized as "Indo-European", have been transformed by local tribal and Dravidian idioms in the course of three millennia. They have been Indianized. We make this observation, here, because during the late 19th and early 20th centuries the European Indologists introduced into the parlance of South Asian elite what today's cynics call the "Aryan myth", which created a rift between two Asian traditions on ethno-linguistic grounds — and this is a well documented event. We, therefore, avoid this baseless dichotomy and regard all these languages as Asian. Besides, they are all permeated by Indic religiousness.

2

By "Western" I mean not only what is Euro-American but often what is characteristically proper to Rome's/Vatican's theological culture; it is the latter that I have in mind whenever I speak of the *Western Patriarchate*. Note that Rome and the West have been accomplices in five centuries of missionary praxis, which our non-Christian fellow Asians interpret, quite justifiably, as *Euro-Ecclesiastical expansionism*. But my insistence on "Asianness" and my tendency to contrast it with what is Western (both Roman and Euro-American) is an historical necessity and not an expression of any antipathy towards the West and its Christianity but for which I would not be a Christian today. Hence I insist that **the term "Asian" as applied to theology in this work reflects the need for *the Christian Kerygma* to be *communicable and intelligible to Asians* in their Semitic, Indic, Sinic, and other languages as well as in Asia's distinctively *religious* idiom.**

Not the content but the *process* of theology
The content of a theology is the same everywhere. But it assumes different contours according to the method employed in theologizing. What engages me in this book is not the content, which I have already published elsewhere, but the *art* or the *technique* of *doing* theology. The word *technique* should be traced back to its original Greek sense of *technē*, which means "art" or the "style" of doing things. The art is not a means to an end. In the competitive world of ours, the *art of playing* a game has ceased to be the ultimate esthetic goal to be enjoyed; it has become the means of indulging in the beastly urge to overpower the other. In music fortunately, style and

3

performance merge. Even the word 'method' is derived from the Greek word *hodos*, the way. The "way" of doing theology cannot be dissociated from the "goal" of theology. He who is the Eternal WORD is also the WAY, which is Salvation. Theology is a *process* of interpreting a *given datum* which is identified here as The WORD; it is not a "system" that emerges at the end of a process. It is the process itself that constitutes a theology. To put it more directly: theology is a synonym for theologizing.

The genesis of this book
The *core thesis* of this book is contained only in PARTS I AND II; all the other chapters are reprints of previously published articles which certainly play an indispensably supplementary role. The core thesis originated as a seminar which I conducted in the Sinhala medium for the post-graduate students of the Department of Western Civilization and Christian Culture at the University of Kelaniya in September 2010. There, I presented an *Asian Liberation Theology* as a *process* that begins, evolves and culminates as a praxis of *obedience to the Word of God* —the Word spoken in the Bible and also incessantly heard in Asia's complex and on-going history, a history which discloses an interplay between the major world religions that have their wellsprings in this continent, on the one hand, and the defective socio-economic structures that have generated the largest concentration of dispossessed persons in the world, on the other.

Hence the kind of **Asian Liberation Theologian** that I envisage in these pages is someone

4

(a) Who *reads and lives the Christian sources of revelation as a Semite-in-spirit*
(b) breathing and *absorbing the ethos of Asia's non-Christian soteriologies*
(c) filtering them through the *aspirations and the struggles of the oppressed masses*.

The locus of theologizing

The shocking experience of the Marxist youth insurrection that took place towards the end of my doctoral studies here in Sri Lanka (April 1971) made me *re-interpret* the profound spiritual transformation I had gone through while practicing meditation under the personal guidance of a Buddhist monk. This led me to imagine that an apostolate of inculcating a socio-spiritual integration in the disadvantaged and disillusioned rural youth —employing various art-forms (music, dance, drama etc.)— would enable me also to create a fresh, lively and esthetically liberating variety of indigenous theology based on a *tasteful* exchange between the country's diverse cultures which are saturated with a vibrant religiousness.

But this dream of mine clashed with my superiors' plans to gradually make Rome the base from where I was to render my apostolic service, not to the youth of Sri Lanka as an itinerant minister, but to the international academe as a globe-trotting Indologist and Theologian,. During my Tertianship (the final formation period of a Jesuit) which I did in India (September 1971), my Tertian Master, Fr Conget advised me to first *obey* my superiors and do a stint of teaching in Rome and *then* evaluate it and offer my own suggestions to them. That is what I did. After a

5

week of discernment under the guidance of Fr Juan Alfaro, my senior colleague at the Gregorian University (Rome), I decided to make *Sri Lanka* (rather than Rome) *the base* from which I could carry out the mission entrusted to me by my superiors: to serve the international academe as an Indologist and Theologian —without neglecting the work among our own rural youth.

My superiors took one year to discuss my proposal and finally mandated me to station myself in a rural village a few miles outside the city of Colombo (within relatively short distance from the Kelaniya University) and do my international apostolate from there. The seminars I conducted for rural youth, (Christian and non-Christian), university students and factory-workers in the vernacular were an impressive *learning process* for me, as was also the field work done specially in 1980s and mentioned in the pages of this book. This Sri Lankan experience was complemented by *another learning process* that I passed through while lecturing in several universities in the world and also holding chairs (professorships) in both Pontifical and Protestant Faculties. Thus **rootedness in the local** and **openness to the global** became for me a *conditio sine qua non* for "learning" the art of theologizing in Asia.

An autobiographical approach
The autobiographical approach I had adopted in the aforementioned seminar is continued here, especially in PART TWO —which explains why I am constrained to quote myself so often from my previous writings. Hence in the first half of the book (Parts I and II) *all references are to my earlier articles and books* unless

6

otherwise indicated. For it is a long personal journey that I recount here in summary form to convince the listeners /readers that this species of activity is within everybody's reach; what I could, all young Asians can. For theology is not an exercise reserved to an exclusive club but the work of a community while the "formal" theologian is the one who interprets, articulates and throws back to the community its own collective visioning as an open-ended project rather than as a close-knit system so that others can continue or change its direction and correct or complete its proposals in response to the signs of the times. My conviction is that the formal theologians walk as perpetual pilgrims on the path that opens up before them each time they converse with the One Who hears and speaks in and outside one's own Holy Writ as well as in and outside one's own ecclesial community.

Though the first study-session was communicated *orally* and in the *vernacular* medium —a principle I defend in these pages as a *sine qua non* for the emergence of a theology that is authentically Asian— I thought of presenting, here, an expanded English version of it for the sake of the wider reading public, while simultaneously preparing the Sinhala original for eventual publication.

The outline of the book
In the two chapters that constitute **PART ONE** of this book, I offer some *theoretical clarifications about a few fundamentals* which are presupposed in the main thesis expounded in Part Two. The reason is that in my input (which I amplify here in English), I had to dismantle certain thought patterns which some of my clerical

7

listeners had inherited from superannuated theologies and catechisms used in traditional ecclesiastical institutions. Hence in this work, too, I anticipate the answers to the same questions that a similar category of readers could raise when perusing this book. However theoretical these preliminary elucidations may sound, they are a hurdle that *must* be cleared before the rest of the book could make sense.

PART TWO contains three chapters in which I assemble all the *principles that govern the art of theologizing* in Asia in the course of an *autobiographical* narrative. This part contains the <u>quintessence of the entire book</u>, and the book, therefore, begins and ends here.

In **PART THREE**, I reproduce two samples from my previous writings to *illustrate* as well as *confirm* the methodology detailed in Part Two.   One chapter introduces an Asian mode of interpreting the Scriptures and the other deals with the Asian understanding of Christ in the context of Religious pluralism.

But the final Chapter, which constitutes **PART FOUR** — also a reprint of a previously published   article— offers a neat *summary* and a quick *review* of the whole work. Here the reader is exposed to a repetition of all the key concepts and arguments that s/he had already met in the first substantial half (Parts I and II) of the book. "Repetition helps" *(repetita juvant)* is a pivotal principle in Ignatian pedagogy !

Aloysius Pieris, s.j.
Tulana Research Centre
Gonawala-Kelaniya, Sri Lanka
January 2013.

8

Part One

Preliminary Clarifications : A Necessary Prelude

CHAPTER 1
Threefold Role of Theology and Theologians:
EXPERIENCING, REMEMBERING AND INTERPRETING LIBERATION

1. Three Moments in Judeo-Christianity

At the Second Inter-Monastic Congress in which I took part as a Resource Person (Bangalore 1973), I heard Raymond Panikkar (another Resource Person) dropping an insight on the audience, almost as an *obiter dictum*, without developing it into a thesis, then or later. He had a knack of throwing seminal ideas during conversations, allowing his hearers to pick up and work out their implications. Hence the following casual remark, which he flung at us during one of his interventions, provided not only a framework for my lectures on comparative study of religions[1] but also a springboard for launching the process of evolving a method of "theologizing" specially at a period of time (1970s) when I had begun to fathom the Asian Reality in terms of a Christocentric

---

[1] See "Comparative Study of Buddhism and Christianity: Notes on Methodology", being Chapter VII in *Prophetic Humour in Buddhism and Christianity : Doing Inter-Religious Studies in the Reverential Mode*, EISD, Colombo, 2005, pp. 105-134. (Hence forward *Prophetic Humour*)

spirituality that I acquired through a regular practice of *lectio divina* and Ignatian Exercises. It is therefore with gratitude that I recall and repeat here Panikkar's lapidary statement :-

"There are **three moments**
in the evolution of *any* religion:-

the EXPERIENCE,
the MEMORY of that experience
and the INTERPRETATION of the memory.
But Truth *lies* in Interpretation".

These were his exact words. In the last sentence he was punning on the two meanings of "lies" in English (*resides* and *distorts*), hinting that inter-religious dialogue could be a hazardous exercise if carried out only at the level of interpretation. All the additional expressions found in the Diagram no. 1 (page 12), including the identification of the third level as "theology", are entirely my own amplification of Panikkar's seminal statement. Hence the array of conclusions that I have drawn below from his passing observation should not be attributed to him, though I am almost certain he would have concurred with my elaborations.

It should be further noted that the schematic version of it indicated in Diagram no. 1 is not only the theoretical *framework* within which I discuss the genesis and the nature of a theology in the pages that follow but also the fundamental *presupposition* in all that I say in this whole work.

11

Diagram 1

Three Moments/Levels
In the Evolution of Christianity

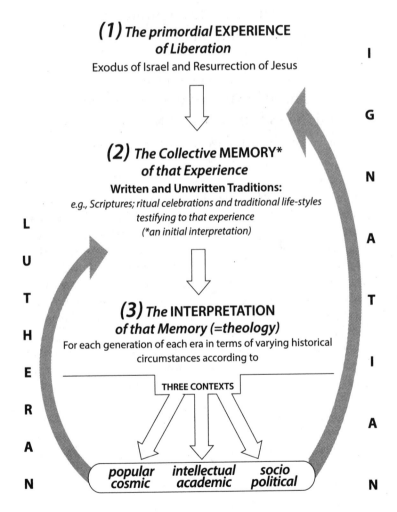

(1) The primordial EXPERIENCE
of Liberation
Exodus of Israel and Resurrection of Jesus

(2) The Collective MEMORY*
of that Experience
Written and Unwritten Traditions:
e.g., Scriptures; ritual celebrations and traditional life-styles
testifying to that experience
*(*an initial interpretation)*

(3) The INTERPRETATION
of that Memory (=theology)
For each generation of each era in terms of varying historical
circumstances according to

THREE CONTEXTS

popular   intellectual   socio
cosmic   academic   political

I G N A T T I A N

L U T H E R A N

Before I comment on this diagram, I would like to modify Panikkar's insightful dictum by pointing out that the Second Moment. i.e., the **"collective memory"** —both written (scriptures) and unwritten (oral traditions and practices)— **is already an initial** *interpretation*, i.e., an attempt at **theologizing!** I say this because the "primordial experience of liberation" is something that is 'remembered', i.e., *mentally verbalized by humans*; and this necessarily implies an epistemic process that *culturally* modifies one's understanding of it. What I mean is that **one cannot** *remember* **an ineffable experience without couching it in the** *cultural* **idiom that has shaped one's thinking and feeling;** such remembrance, therefore, is a species of inchoative "interpretation" or a seminal theology. This is what the Scriptures are in most religions.

We observe this phenomenon in comparative mysticism. The ecstasy that a Christian mystic such as Teresa of Avila describes, employing the idiom of "conjugal union" proper to the "agapeic" language of her religious tradition, **seems to be a similar experience of supreme joy** (resulting from total detachment) that the Buddhist Nuns sing about in the *Therīgāthā* (The Psalms of the Sisters) but have expressed in the "gnostic" idiom, i.e., as a mental "realization" of the cessation of *all* unions including the conjugal union! Nirvana is *yogakkhema*, "freedom from every bond".[2] A liberational experience defies human language and therefore cannot be remembered (i.e. mentally verbalized) except in one's religio-cultural idiom, whose mediation, therefore, is an *interpretation*. This means there can be two successive or even simultaneous interpretations of the same experience. This is eminently true of the Written Word in Christianity

---

[2] Here *yoga* means union and *khema* signifies release or freedom. In Buddhism it means release from every form of union which is a bond of attachment; on the other hand other Indic spiritualities could read the opposite meaning : "Freedom through Union".

13

which does not claim that the revelatory words were *verbatim* dictated by God, in contrast with Islam's claim that the Koran contains Allah's *ipsissima verba,* and against a similar claim made quite naively in Leo XIII's *Providentissimus Deus* —fortunately to be offset decades later in Pius XII's *Divino Afflante Spiritu.*

We believe that the Bible is inspired, i.e., written under the influence of God's Breath, who is a divine Person. By this I mean that the inspired compliers have *interpreted* their national history from God's point of view, reading Her Word in all that happened. To bring this concept out I have invented the neologism *Theography of Israel* or God's Story in the story of a People covenanted with God, as I explain in Chapter V (pp.143-144). A reading of these same books in the light of the Eternal Word made flesh as Jesus Christ has produced the New Testament which again is a *theography* of the New Israel.

The implication of this observation is that our entire **Christian Patrimony** consisting of the *scriptures of both covenants and various traditional practices*, which constitute the Collective Memory (of the primordial experience of liberation), include many interpretations or *theologies.* For *human words* which constitute Scriptures are a *memory* of the ineffable revelatory-redemptive experience; that is to say they are (humanly) "remembered" (i.e., "interpreted") versions of a primordial salvific event that defies accurate transposition into a human discourse. Despite human limitations these words (Sprit–inspired human *interpretations* of the primordial experience) are the means which the Nascent Christian Community has offered its members (past present and future) as a stepping stone for touching the "Transcendent" (i.e., *The Word* which hides behind these human words). Such intepretations are all, therefore, *theologies.*

14

Each of the four gospels, which form the core of Christian Scriptures can also be cited as a *scriptural exercise in theologizing*, for they are each a double *interpretation* of the Christ Event experienced by the nascent church —the first being the accounts of those who remembered the encounter with Jesus, and the second the evangelists' fourfold narrative based on those oral accounts. The book of Deuteronomy in the OT is another typical example. Jewish scholars refer to this book as "an interpretation of scripture", i.e., an "inner-biblical exegesis" constituting a legitimate   part of the biblical tradition.[3]

A theologian, therefore, has to study these *given* interpretations (or theologies) contained within the Written and Unwritten Memory as *biblical models of theologizing*. The Scriptures, therefore, are a *library of theologies* besides being the *door to the primordial liberative* event from which they originated. Which means that besides being a **repository of The Word** (i.e. the revelation of an ineffable experience of liberation), they are also the prime **school of theology** wherin the art of interpreting Revelation is taught.

One final clarification:- "theology" which we have defined as the "interpretation of The Word" should not be confused with the *hermeneutical science* normally referred to as *exegesis* which, in our vocabulary, is not "interpretation" as such but an "interpretational technique" (tools as well as method) needed for understanding a sacred text and communicating it to one's contemporaries. This observation will be further clarified in Chapter VI.

---

[3] Everett Fox, *The Five Books of Moses*, Shocken Books Inc., Random House New York, 1995 (Fourth Edition), p. 844 (citing M. Fishbane, *Biblical Interpretation in Ancient Israel*, Oxford 1988).

15

2. Scripture and Tradition as "Written and Unwritten Memory of a Liberative Experience"

I am happy that the debate between Protestants and Catholics on the relationship between "scripture and tradition" has been mildly resolved by the Bishops and Theologians of Vatican II in its document on Revelation, *Verbum Dei*. However, Asians would have a better way of treating these two elements as one indivisible Source if they subsume them under the rubric of the *Collective Memory* of the Primordial Experience of Liberation. The presupposition is that all **"metacosmic"** religions have *a primordial experience of liberation* as their origin, e.g. the Buddha's and Mahavira's Nirvana in **Buddhism** and **Jainism** respectively, YHWH's salvific intervention or Exodus in **Judaism**, the Resurrection of Jesus in **Christianity**, Allah's revelation to **Mohamed** in Islam, the *Advaita*-experience of sages in the **Vedanta** tradition. Their **sacred texts** and **oral traditions** together constitute their *collective memory*. The Hindus refer to them as *śruti* and *smṛti* respectively. Others treat the sacred texts as *sūtra* and their interpretations as *śāstra*. The **"cosmic"** or primal religions, too, arise from a *pancosmic ecopathy* with the sacred powers of Nature which are remembered and celebrated through a fusion of narratives and rituals that are transmitted *orally* to subsequent generations.[4]

Take, for instance, the *Exodus*, the liberation of Israel from slavery. It was something much more than just a group of slaves physically escaping from Egypt to a state of independence and national sovereignty. Rather, it was an indescribable in-depth experience of the impossible taking place right in their presence thanks to an awesome encounter with Some One *revealed* as YHWH whom the later generations would call affectionately "God of Womb-Love" (*'El-raḥūm*) and "God of Unconditional Love" (*'El-ḥanūn*),

---

[4] There is an entire excursus on *cosmic religion* in Chapter IV.

because this God was *experienced* as being deeply hurt by the their suffering and moved by compassion to join them in their struggle. They *remembered* this revelatory event not only through a repetition of "discourses, narratives, poetry and parables" that have been *written down* later but also through various "symbolic acts" such as the celebration of the Passover, the Pentecost, the Feast of Booths and so on, which have been passed on orally from generation to generation —though, no doubt, they too could be and had been transposed into a written format in a subsequent era.

The *Resurrection* of Jesus or the Risen Jesus was the other indescribable and yet **foundational experience** of **liberation** that is **remembered** in the NT ("Scripture") as well as in practices such as the sacramental celebration of the paschal mystery ("Tradition"). Hence the **Collective Memory** contains both **written and unwritten** interpretations (or theologies) that have been handed down together with the **praxis** by means of which the believers were "bearing witness" to this extraordinary salvific intervention as recurring in their lives. **Scripture and tradition are not two currents but one stream of continuous *memory*.** Memory (*zkr*) is the key word here.

Cardinal Thomas Spidlik, s.j. insists, following St Basil, that the spirituality of the Bible is *not an act of contemplation* (in the tradition of the Greeks) *but an act of* **remembrance** (in the tradition of the Jews).[5] The same can be said of the way the New Testament records the disciples' *memory* of Jesus, his life and works, his words and deeds, and specially his death and rising. That is why the **Holy Eucharist**, one of the items of an unwritten tradition that makes us *recall* or bring

---

[5] Thomas Spidlik, s.j., *Prayer: Spirituality of the Christian East*, Volume 2, Cistercian Publications, Kalamazoo, Michigan (2005), pp. 263-265.

to *memory* these events, is called *anamnesis* (remembering).[6] The Eucharist, in other words, is a continuous remembrance (*anamnesis*) of the Christ-Event in the "Eternal Now" of God wherein everything that happened through Christ from creation to consummation is recalled and celebrated by the whole Christian community. Hence this sacramental *anamnesis* has to be complemented by an *anamnesis* of another kind on the part of the formal **theologian,** for his role is to *sustain this collective memory by interpreting it* in such a way as to make it *accessible to each generation* in the cultural, linguistic, social and political idiom of that generation.

Note further that, since theology is essentially an *interpretation* of the memory of a liberational experience, it is invariably a *liberation theology;* there cannot be a theology that is not liberational. Hence the phrase "liberation theology" is a tautology, which we are, nevertheless, constrained to employ in our formal discourses in order to contrast authentic theologies from those that are predominantly rational "systems".

3. Necessity and Variety of "Theologies" (or "Interpretations")
It is not difficult to see why *The Word* needs to be *decoded* and *re-interpreted* to each new generation in response to the *ever changing socio-historical circumstances.* Minus this exercise, the primordial experience as well as its collective memory cannot make any sense to or have any impact on contemporary society. In fact many religions (such as the

---

[6] For which I have coined the word *parismṛti / parismaraṇa* in my mother tongue and it can be appropriated by many other Indic languages. This neologism is not found in any Sanskrit dictionary. I coined it on the analogy of the frequently used Sanskrit term *anusmṛti* (recalling a past event which remains a past event). By using the prefix *pari* in place of *anu,* I try to convey the sense of the Hebrew technical term *zkr* to indicate a remembrance that participates *here and now* in the past event as well as its future completion; that is an entry into the redemptive events in the *Eternal Now* of God in the celebration of the Eucharist.

Egyptian, the Mesopotamian) have disappeared from history partly because their adherents had failed to indulge in continuous interpretation of the Collective Memory for the benefit of successive generations in creative response to changing socio-cultural circumstances. This is eminently true of certain forms of traditional Christianity tenaciously clung to in the Western Patriarchate's Central Bureau but unintelligible to the modern generation. Reading afresh and re-interpreting the Collective Memory (or the written and unwritten Word) in response to the socio-historical reality that we meet in various parts of the world in these our times is what *we* understand by "new evangelization" and what John XXIII meant by *aggiornamento*. An *ongoing* interpretation is absolutely necessary for any religion to survive the vicissitudes of times and climes. Theologizing, in other words, is not at all a once-and-for-all task.

Furthermore, it is our contention that no theology can be comprehensively evangelical and catechetically effective unless it is an interpretation of THE WORD in *all the three contexts* which I have enumerated above in Diagram no. 1 (p. 12):- the *popular-cosmic, the intellectual-academic and socio-political.* Each is a *context* for theologizing but each needs to be complemented by the other two. Unfortunately, we have inherited a notion of theology that is too narrowly circumscribed by intellectual-academic elaborations and therefore we suffer from the false impression that a theologian is necessarily one who uses sophisticated philosophical tools to analyze and build up a rationally demonstrable system of thought. This is because the traditional scholastic theology is still held by some as *the* standard paradigm of theologizing. Hence most academicians have failed to critically study the implicit theologies of poets and painters, the creators of the popular religious theatre, the makers of films and the message of ancient story-telling sages. (See Chapter V for a comprehensive discussion on this suggestion)

In fact, one who is deeply committed to Christ and seeks to deepen one's understanding of that personal faith and witnesses to it in one's *personal life* as well as in on one's *social commitments*, has already spelt out a *theopraxis* which is the first formulation of a theology. It is in this sense that we can speak of the theology of a Benedict, a Francis, an Ignatius, a Teresa and so on in the Roman church, or a Calvinistic, a Lutheran and a Wesleyan theology in the Reformed churches. They are each one particular person's appropriation and articulation of an implicit tradition discovered in the ecclesial community rather than an idiosyncratic achievement of an individual. I am happy that one of my dreams came true when Christopher Pramuk, in response to my suggestion relayed to him by Tim Burk, s.j., produced a solid thesis on the Christology of Thomas Merton, a great Western theologian whose heart and mind were saturated with Asian sensitivity.[7]

Hence it follows that *one* of the tasks of Asia's "formal" theologians is to recognize, appropriate and name such implicit theologies and eventually to express them in a catechetically effective and socially transformative manner. This is specially true of the contents of my book *An Asian Theology of Liberation* that has been too hastily attributed to me, for I did not invent it but *discovered* it in the Asian Reality in which I immersed myself with a biblical mindset and *articulated* it in various ways. In fact this is the story I am narrating in **PART II** (Chapters III, IV and V) of this work to illustrate the genesis of a theology!

---

[7] C. Pramuk, *Sophia, The Hidden Christ of Thomas Merton,* Liturgical Press, Colgeville , Minnesota, USA, 2009.

4. The Three Inseparable Contexts: Popular, Philosophical and Political

The "popular theologies" arise from the *common people's praxis of their faith*, which reveals an implicit interpretation of their religiosity in terms of the needs of the *here and now*. The day-to-day problems such as economic constraints, marital problems, health questions, social relationships, cosmic disasters, are the foremost concerns in what we call *cosmic religions* or "primal religions" as manifested in clannic and tribal or shamanic societies of the world; this same species of religiosity has become the matrix in which the basic tenets of the major (meta-cosmic) religions are practised by the ordinary masses. Thus for instance, Latin America's so-called "Popular Christianity", which is expressed in the language of indigenous beliefs and practices, is also a species of theology. There is a value to be recognized in the *this-worldly* approach which such popular interpretations adopt. It challenges the pie-in-the-sky theology of abstract theorizers. That is why the Catholic Asian bishops (FABC Papers, no. 81) have quite rightly criticized the misplaced missionary zeal that tried to destroy the primal forms of religiousness in Asia as superstition. I discuss this species of cosmic religiosity in greater detail in Chapter IV.

Secondly, there is also the level of "rational investigation and intellectual justification", wherein the aforementioned "abstract" theories *could* and *do* often occur. Many traditional theologies, in their past and present forms, are scholastic interpretations of Revelation in terms of human *Reason*. They are born of the zeal to reconcile **faith and reason**. Our task, on the contrary, is to proclaim the biblical emphasis on the intimate nexus between **faith and *justice***. Hence, let me insist *ad nauseam* that theology is not "faith seeking understanding" (*fides quaerens intellectum*) but "faith promoting justice" (*fides promovens justitiam*). The

21

rational approach is not denied but is made to subserve "the holding together of the service of faith and the promotion of justice".[8]

Unfortunately, the scholastic form prevalent in the Western Patriarchate since at least the medieval times is sometimes replaced, here in Asia, by indigenous versions of the same species, that is to say, by theologies that strive to dialogue and resonate with the highly speculative philosophies of non-Christian metacosmic religions. They, too, are a *genre* of scholastic theology: *fides quaerens intellectum*. Hence I should clarify, here, that I am not criticizing the traditional scholastic theology because it is Western, but because it has deviated from the primordial experience and collective memory by relying too much on a philosophical system, just like some of the Asian theologies, alluded to above. It is the methodology of that theology that I question here; not its provenance!

The so-called "systemicity" or "coherentism" in theology such as recognized in contemporary Thomism and post-Thomistic scholasticism by its many defenders, is being questioned, here, on the ground that we are dealing with a Transcendental Mystery which always leaves 'gaps' so that we can never cramp it into a rational construct. That is why I would not absolutize "dogmas" which are but human artifacts that can only be an *aid* to our faith rather than the *object* of our faith.[9] For there is a receding horizon to be accepted as "a given" in the realm of the Word of Salvation that is revealed as the object of our obedience. Hence I am not anti-

---

[8] As elaborated in "Re-visiting the Faith-Justice Mission :One More Appeal for a Paradigm Shift", *Third Millennium*, January 2012, pp. 6-20. For a revised reprint, see *Our Unhidden Agenda, How We Jesuits Work, Pray and Form our Men*, TMU, Kelaniya, 2012, pp.20-35. **(Hence forward *Our Hidden Agenda*)**
[9] See "Dogmas, Faith and God's Word: Eleven Irksome Questions for the Year of Faith", *Vāgdevī, Journal of Religious Reflection*, Kelaniya, Sri Lanka no. 12, July 2012, pp. 41-65. **(Hence forward *Vāgdevī*)**

intellectual (or else I would not be arguing my case in this manner); I am simply being cautious about the limits of the human reason when it comes to both the *practice* and the *profession* of our Faith.[10] Our contention is that any systematic and logically coherent thinking, which is *not* firmly rooted in a praxis leading to liberation, is a species of *diṭṭhi* ("soteriologically inconsequential speculation") as the Buddha had pointed out, for this great Asian Sage understood truth soteriologocally rather than rationally, or much less, rationalistically.[11] In fact this Asian approach bears some affinity to the Patristic one. For theology is not a mere rational *explanation* of our faith but a dynamic involvement of the minds and hearts of a faith-community in the *transformation* of this present existence into God's Reign of love and justice, as will be discussed in more detail in Chapter V (pp.131-137).

Finally we come to "political theologies", which are of at least two kinds: "liberation theologies" and "domination theologies". The latter bear the marks of certain political ideologies and social organizational models such as feudalism, colonialism, and so on and the concomitant policy of imposing the intruder's culture, religion and even language on the conquered nations. This species of missiology was taken for granted in the church till Vatican II as I demonstrate in Chapter IV (pp.122-123). Even some of the aforementioned "inculturated theologies" churned out in an Indic context are criticized today by the members of the non-Brahmanic oppressed classes or "scheduled castes" as a Christian justification of Brahmanic domination and a patriarchal duplication of the West's domination theologies.

---

[10] I continue this discussion in Chapter II Section 3 (pp. 37-40)
[11] As demonstrated with textual evidence in "Truth and Freedom in the Tripitaka and the Bible: Towards an Inter-Scriptural Dialogue", *Dialogue, NS,* (Ecumenical Institute, Colombo) vols. xxxv-xxxvi (2008-2009), pp.160-180. (**Hence forward** *Dialogue, NS*)

23

By contrast, 'liberation theologies' —as evident from their varied Asian forms such as Minjung theology, Dalit theology, Asian feminist theology and so on— dovetail with the *this-worldly* spirituality of *cosmic religions* while resonating with the liberative teachings of metacosmic religions, which are seen as soteriologies or so many paths of salvation.[12] Asian theologies of liberation treat other metacosmic religions not as rivals in a conversion race but as fellow-pilgrims collaborating in a common mission —obviously complementing them with the *this-worldly spirituality of cosmic religions* (as explained in Chapters III and IV).

4. The *Risks* of Interpretations and the Need for *Safeguards*

Let us learn a lesson from what happened to the medieval European theology which St Thomas Aquinas, guided by Providence, created in response to a particular intellectual challenge that the church faced when Aristotelian philosophy was imported to Europe by Islamic theologians in a form that questioned the philosophical validity of Christianity. The Angelic Doctor (taking the mantle from St Albert, the Great) responded to the *signs of the times* by producing an intellectually respectable alternative to the ineffective and outmoded theology that prevailed till then. It was an *interpretation* of the Word at the academic-rational level (the second type of context mentioned at level 3 in Diagram I). It became *the* official theology of the Roman church after facing an initial resistance and even hostility on the part of the hierarchy; unfortunately, however, it remained *the* theology of the church even after it had ceased to serve its purpose owing to changes in Europe's socio-cultural contexts! Let me explain this event in greater detail:-

---

[12] See my "Political Theologies in Asia" in : Peter Scott & William T. Cavanaugh (eds.), *The Blackwell Companion to Political Theology,* Blackwell Publishing Company,, 2003, pp. 256-270.

By mid-19th century, a *re-interpretation of Thomism* —rather than a new interpretation of *The Word* in response to the changing social context—seemed to have taken place when the scientific and rational systems of thought which began to pervade Western Europe had challenged the Thomistic system. This re-interpreted and re-confirmed Thomism (sometimes known as *Neo-Thomism* or neo-scholasticism), was defended and endorsed by the Western Patriarch (Leo XIII, *Aeterni Patris,* August 1879) as the official philosophical basis for theologizing, which, therefore, was expected to be taught in all Catholic Seminaries —including, of course, those in Asia. When its limitations were once more exposed by new challenges specially in the 20th century, the response was *another re-interpretation of Thomism.* Thus emerged "Transcendent Thomism", sarcastically nicknamed *Nouvelle Theologie* by the conservative wing of Neo-Thomists led by Reginald Marie Garrigou-LaGrange.

I beg not to be misunderstood here. I do acknowledge with immense gratitude that it was the advocates of *Nouvelle Theologie* who indulged in a return to the Collective Memory (*reditus ad fontes* in Latin and *ressourcement* in French) and prepared the *Western Church* for Vatican II and saved this Council from being hijacked by a minority of diehard conservatives.[13] On the other hand the majority of our Asian Bishops who attended Vatican II were, *on the whole,* mere learner-spectators, although in the post-Conciliar decades some bishops and theologians of our continent —while being grateful to the progressive branch of Neo-Thomism for salvaging the Council from becoming a repetition of Trent or Vatican I— realized that this *Nouvelle Theologie* was *not* radical enough to serve the churches of the *non-Western World.* For, it was not a fresh interpretation of the Word in

---

[13] As explained in my *Providential Timeliness of Vatican II: A Long Overdue Halt to a Scandalous Millennium,* Kelaniya, Sri Lanka 2013 pp. 50-52; 65-68.

the light of the "Modern World", *which is a larger reality than the First World*, but only a reinterpretation of an interpretation made within the European context. Even today the secularized and de-churched West is waiting to be served by a theology that is capable of responding to its dilemmas. Which makes Benedict XVI's zeal for a New Evangelization of Europe a mere pipedream. The failure to take the *new* reality as a God-given context and the failure to re-read God's Word within that *new* context, as illustrated in the two foregoing examples (Thomism and Neo-Thomism), constitutes the **first risk** in theologizing. For a well crystallized theological tradition could become a thing of the past.

The second risk is connected with the **spatio-temporal distance** that separates theology (Level Three) from both the primordial experience (Level One) and its memory (Level Two). The theologian must never forget that every contemporary theology can deteriorate into a self-contained "system" cut off from the first two moments of the religious experience, and thus cease to be a soteriology or a path of liberation. In fact a theology that does not originate from, resonate with and incessantly mediate *liberation* (i.e., the originating experience) cannot be a theology. As we remarked earlier, it is either liberation theology or no theology!

Thus the 16th century's *scholastic theology* (a deterioration of the medieval Thomism with its Aristotelian framework) had travelled so far away from the Primordial Experience (i.e., the Encounter with the Crucified-Risen Christ) as well as from its Written and Unwritten Memory (i.e., Scripture and Tradition) that Ignatius of Loyola lamented that his theological studies at Paris had dried up his heart spiritually. Hence he sought hard to recapture the **primordial liberative experience** (*Level One*), whereas Martin Luther with a

26

similar reaction towards that same sterile theology tried to return to the **Scriptures** (*Level Two*). This is what *reditus ad fontes* ("Back to the Sources" or *ressourcement*) means. I have indicated this in Diagram no. 1 (p.12) in the form of *two upward moving shaded arrows.* The principle I wish to emphasize here is that just as the Scriptures are the "soul of theology" as Vatican II has declared (*DV,*24), so too, the primordial experience is the "soul of the Scriptures". Put it differently, theology (level three) is animated by the Collective Memory (level two) which, in its turn is animated by the Primordial Experience (level one).

Hence, as a **safeguard** against this two-fold risk (i.e., a theology becoming outdated in view of changing historical circumstances, on the one hand, and becoming detached and distanced from the Primordial Experience and its Memory, on the other), the theologians must develop a method of **incessant involvement with Contemporary Reality** (third level) **as well as an incessant recourse to the Experience and its Memory** (first two levels). A constant recourse to scriptures (level two), as Luther did, and an attempt to be in constant touch with the primordial liberational experience (level one), as Ignatius did, is an *obligation* that no Asian theologian can afford to neglect.

To sum up: The on-going reference to the first two levels (experience and memory) is the guarantee of *orthodoxy* in every theology, while the ongoing critical response to ever-changing social reality is the guarantee of its *contemporary relevance.* Both *orthodoxy* and *relevance* are essential features of an authentic theology.[]

CHAPTER II
"Before the Bible was, I am"
THE WORD OF GOD AND THE
WRITTEN COLLECTIVE MEMORY

1. Christ as the Word of God

Before I discuss the process of theologizing in Asia (in PART TWO), I have to dispel a grave misconception prevalent among various churches about the "Word of God". It is true that all "happenings" or events and even evil ones of our own making could become a vehicle of God's communication with us. It is true that David's adultery or Jacob's duplicity is not God's Word (i.e., it is not what "God wills" for us); nevertheless God has issued a mission-cum-message, i.e., "a word-command" (*dābār*) to us through those sinful events. It is only in this broad sense that even the inhuman and sinful act of torturing and crucifying Jesus is referred to in the NT as the Will (i.e., the executive *word*) of God, though God never wills suffering and death for any person, just as She did not will David's adultery or Jacob's duplicity. Interestingly, the Bible often employs the term "words" (*dᵉbārîm*) as a synonym for *events, things* or *happenings*. In that sense, everything that exists and happens is a "word of God" because there is always a divine message-cum-mission conveyed in it. The implication, if properly understood, is that all words are deeds and all deeds are words to those who believe in Her who is God of Moses and Father of Jesus. In that sense the Bible is *super-eminently a* word of God —

28

'word' with *simple* 'w', i.e., a mission-cum-message that has come into existence with God's knowledge and will.

On the other hand, I am taken aback when the infelicitous statement that the "Scriptures are *the* Word of God" (Word with Capital 'W') is heard and read or at least implied not infrequently even where greater precision is expected —by which I mean some official church documents as well as in theological treatises of some scholars. For if we push this equation to its logical conclusion we end up with the idolatrous stance that the fundamentalists hold and advocate. Hence the following lengthy clarification:-

The Bible is *not* "*The* Word of God". **Christ** alone is God's Eternal Word, a communicative happening that solicits a response. The Bible is only a book, albeit a book of a unique kind that commands all the reverence due to a sacred object precisely because it is *a privileged locus* where Christ, the Eternal Word is heard and encountered. That is why "The church has always venerated the divine Scriptures as it has venerated the Body of the Lord" (*DV,* 21). On the other hand the tendency to equate the Bible with *The* Word leads one to bibliolatry, the worship of a book with all that it says, falling into a *literalism* that distorts that divine Word which is **Christ**. For the recognition of Jesus as God's Sovereignty —both the Reign and the Regnant, the King and the Kingdom— visualized as the Ascension, is the basis of our understanding of him as the Christ: a shorthand for God's Reign enfleshed in Jesus who, as the Risen Christ is gathering all things into himself —*the* Revealer-Saviour who is at the same time the Revelation-Salvation. Thus in Christianity's theological vocabulary, the term "Christ" has become a synonym for **the plenitude of salvation and revelation.** It is in this sense that the post-Easter Christians led by John and Paul believed Jesus to be the Christ. In other religions, we Christians can detect homologues for It, such

29

as *Tathatā, Sanāthana Dharma, Dao,* and so on, which, of course, these other-religionists would not apply to Jesus.

Hence we maintain that the "plenitude of salvation and revelation" —which *we* Christians name 'Christ' and which coincides with the Primordial Experience of Liberation mediated by and coinciding with Jesus dead-risen-ascended— is precisely what is *revealed* in the process of being *remembered* in the Bible. Wherefore the Bible is *not* the plenitude of salvation and revelation, but is the place we can encounter It; nor is the Bible the one and only repository of the plenitude of revelation and salvation. **"Before the Bible was, I am"**! The One who is the plenitude of revelation and salvation exists not only *before* the Bible was compiled but also *outside* the biblical world. Furthermore the Bible, as I shall develop further in the discussion below, is also *a divine pedagogy* in that its attentive readers are provided with a chance of being trained to recognize that "plenitude of salvation and revelation" wherever It happens both within and even outside the biblical texts as well as in and outside the community of believers (Israel or the Church).

Note, therefore, the distinction that the sacred writer draws between **Jesus** "in the days of the flesh" and **Christ** "as we know him now" (Heb. 5:7; 2 Cor 5: 16). Let me insist, here, that 'distinction' does not mean 'dichotomy' ! For Jesus (of history) and the Christ (of faith) are inseparable as the Fourth Gospel would have us understand. When we confess that "**JESUS** (in the days of his flesh) **IS THE CHRIST** (as we know him now)" we profess merely that the **whole of Jesus** *is* **the Christ** (i.e., the plenitude of revelation and salvation) **—** *not* **that Jesus is the whole of Christ.** *Totus Jesus est Christus sed Jesus non est totum Christi.* (see diagram no. 2 page 33). For Christhood encompasses the historical person of Jesus *plus* more; for Jesus is joined by many *other providential co-mediators,* including us.

30

This is what we mean when we in Asia declare, to the consternation of our brothers assisting the Central Bureau of the Western Patriarch, that there are other redeemers, that is to say, that Jesus is not the only savior. There is a biblical basis for this assertion in the confession attributed to Paul that his own sufferings had supplemented the redemptive sufferings of Christ, in that he was able to "fill up those things that are **wanting** of the **sufferings** of **Christ**, in my flesh, for his body, which is the church" (Col. 1:24). **Jesus has generously left room for our own contribution to his salvific mission** rather than treat us as passive recipients of a salvation which is forced upon us. Thus there is no reason for alarm when we in Asia speak of Jesus entertaining other co-mediators of redemption.[14] The same scripturally founded observation made above can be reformulated with reference to Jesus the Word of God. **Jesus is entirely God's Word (which is Christ) but Jesus is *not the entirety* of Christ or the Totality of the Word of God,** for there are other revelatory and redemptive words which, together with Jesus, form the *Total Word,* which/whom *we* Christians *name* "Christ".

Note further that when we say salvation is in the *name* of Jesus, we understand 'name' not as a label we tag on to some other reality (as in our languages), but in the biblico-Semitic sense of the *supreme salvific Reality Itself* which is what we name "Christ". When we say "Holy be your Name" we declare that we ardently desire that our Maternal Father's Divine Selfhood be recognized everywhere by every person and nation! It is Christ —the Divine Reality which Jesus is— that Peter refers to when he says , "And by his faith in his

---

[14] Intriguingly, those who are most indignant about this assertion of ours are precisely those same persons who have had no inhibition in lobbying for a dogmatic definition of Mary as a *mediatrix* of the redemption wrought by Christ, i.e., a *co-redemptrix*!

name, *his name itself* has made this [cripple] man strong" (Acts 3: 16). The *name* of Jesus, i.e., "the saving reality that Jesus constitutes" coincides with his Christhood, the plenitude of revelation and salvation. That *Reality*, which we name "Christ" is [the medium as well as the agent of] both revelation and salvation.

Incidentally, this is something that I could not clearly express in a public conversation I had with Dr Wolfhart Pannenberg at the Moedling theological colloquium in the summer of 1986, which was transmitted through the Viennese Radio. Whoever listens to the broadcast would realize that I was speaking of this **Salvific-Revelatory Reality**, without identifying It either as "Christ" or as "Jesus"; but my interlocutor, clearly scandalized and shocked by what *he* understood me to be saying, reacted agitatedly, repeating the words "salvation is only in the *name* of Jesus"! I had not even mentioned as yet the name of Jesus (as the recording clearly proves) nor had I until then named that salvific reality as "Christ". It was going to be my next step. He had jumped ahead. Fearing to hurt his susceptibilities and those of others who shared them, I refrained from speaking further, and my silence was later construed as inability to respond rather than as reluctance to hurt! But the text of the debate is available for reference, though it was not published allegedly at the request of Dr Pannenberg. (I have matured over the years and now I argue back politely and firmly as evidenced in many controversies since then!). What I was restrained from expressing verbally in that colloquium in Austria, is what I indicate diagrammatically as follows:-

32

Diagram 2

Hence these two conclusions:-

(a) **Every** [Christian] **theology is essentially a Christology**, being an interpretation of Christ — God's Word— who is heard not only in the Hebrew-Christian Scriptures but also in the contemporary Asian Reality, which includes many soteriologies, many scriptures and many millions of dispossessed persons awaiting liberation. This is why I speak of a "Liberation Christology of Religious pluralism" in Chapter VII. Since our dear brothers in the Western Patriarchy (the Vatican) still think in terms of the traditional Western theology (which is an *interpretation* based on a medieval European context, a context that has disappeared into the past and is also *far removed* from the Collective Memory of the Primordial Experience), we are constrained to make an ardent appeal to them that our claim —that Jesus is not the one and only redeemer/ revealer but that Jesus himself co-opts *us* (and many others) as his co-redemptive and co-revelatory partners— does not go counter to the Written Memory of our Faith.

33

(b) Christology and Mariology are inseparable. For **Mary is the *model Asian liberation theologian* that we wish to emulate** because, as the prototype and first member of the church (.i.e., essentially a church of the poor), she was the first to recognize the Word, hear It, receive and even conceive It, ponder over It, obey It while letting It grow in her before presenting It to others, declaring, in her *Magnificat,* the central theme of a liberation theology. Hers was *not* an academician's "faith seeking understanding" *(fides quaerens intellectum)* but *a poor and humble woman's* "faith aspiring for liberation" *(fides sperans salutem)* —to adapt a thought borrowed from the Vatican II Mariology :- "She stood out conspicuously *among the Lord's humble and poor ones,* who, **with faith** *(cum fiducia),* **hope for** and receive **salvation** from Him" *(LG 55,* my translation, with emphases added). I return to this theme in greater detail in No. 5 below (p. 43).

2.The Bible as a Manual of Divine Pedagogy

A few years ago, a Chinese Buddhist nun and some monks were sent to me to study Sanskrit in the English medium, since the Sanskrit classes in the university were conducted in Sinhala. They were quite reserved at first, perhaps because they did not know how to relate to a Christian clergyman; gradually the ice was broken, specially after sharing lunch with me at the end of the weekly classes (which regrettably I could not continue). So they became friendly enough to tell me honestly what Christianity really seemed in their eyes! Let me sum up from memory what the Venerable Bhikkhunī Chetana said:-

Hemmed in by the communist ideology in China, I (then, a girl in the teens) was attracted to religion and therefore went in search of a religion that

34

would answer my spiritual needs; and since Buddhism, Daoism, Confucianism etc. were all at hand, I wanted to explore the unknown. So I managed to procure a Bible and started reading it. What a horrible experience that was! I was thoroughly disillusioned and scandalized and even disgusted when I realized that I could not or would not read some of its contents in the company of my own sister. What kind of a *religious* book is this? Wars, fights, murder, violence, revenge, adultery, incest, land-robbing... name an obscenity and it is described there! [...] I found my peace renouncing secular life and becoming a Buddhist nun.

She was not far away from the Truth. What she quite rightly posed as a problem for Buddhist readers was in fact the solid basis of the Christian's faith-response to the Biblical narratives. The Rev. Bhikkhuni Chetana's objection alludes to the **true identity of Christianity**. My brief explanation given to her that day can be expanded as follows:-

God gave us the history of one people, Israel, (a history *interpreted* in the Bible as a story of God's redemptive intervention in the lives of *that* People) in order to train us to *listen to God's voice* heard in the human affairs of *that* particular nation — which was a mixture of good and evil as the history of every nation is even today— so that we could recognize that same God's voice in *our* own personal as well as our national and world history, which is not different from that of Israel but is equally a *locus* of a divine encounter. For the Bible reveals a God who is involved with us in all the things that happen around us through our own decisions, both virtuous and vicious. The inspired writers have rewritten their story from God's point of view, so that we are educated to understand God's role in human affairs.

35

Now, all the horrible things that one reads in that history recorded in the Bible has happened and are happening also in modern history in every country. The Bible teaches that we cannot find this God, the *Summum Bonum* of Christianity, by running away from what happens around us, good and bad. This is where Christianity *differs* radically from Buddhism and other knowledge-oriented religions —by which I do not intend to disparage such religions but simply indicate an instance where they are radically and perhaps irreconcilably *different*. Religious pluralism implies non-negotiable differences among various faiths. Given *our* understanding of the Bible, however, the things recorded in it do not scandalize us because they are true to life and they help us to *face life as it really is today in our national history* wherein we have learnt to hear, recognize and obey God's Word thanks to the training we receive through a *constant meditative reading of that same Bible.*

Hence we treat the Bible as the sacred locus, a privileged sanctuary where that *Word of God, who is Christ,* can be encountered by a prayerful reader of the true-to-life events woven into a story of Israel's struggle to be a People of God. What for? That we may recognize that same Word in contemporary history, obey It, live It and proclaim It *prophetically.* To put it in restricted terms of our human language, the Bible is where the Divine Breath, by which God, so to say, "uttered" *The Word,* also assists the attentive reader to listen and respond to that Word as "God's humanly recognizable Voice". This ancient exercise of prayerful reading was known in the Latin church as *lectio divina* ("reading God" in the Bible), and in the Greek church as *theia anagnosis* ("recognizing or discerning God" in the Bible).

The ideal form of *lectio divina* or *theia anagnosis* takes place when **the Church** assembles around the Table of the Word

36

and the Table of the Bread specially on Sundays and solemn feast days to celebrate the mysteries of Christ. For as the Christian People of God, we are continuous with **the Church** that *formed and presented* the **Written Word** in its normative [or canonical] version to be understood in the light of the **Unwritten Word** (tradition) which, too we have inherited as our patrimony. This manner of "Ecclesially Reading God in the Scriptures", which presupposes an ability to *interpret* the Written and Unwritten Word, imposes on the pastors the obligation to receive a *biblical formation* over and above the usual *courses on Scriptures*; i.e., learn to read the Bible as Semites in spirit and as obedient listeners of Christ, the Word.

Finally, this species of traditional **reading-and-listening exercise** trains us to *recognize* and *obey* that same God's Voice heard here and now in our contemporary history, which includes *the scriptures of other religions*. For God's Eternal Word, the plenitude of revelation and salvation, which is called "Christ" in *our* vocabulary, cannot and should not be restricted to the Bible; that Voice is heard everywhere. We must, therefore, be grateful to God for having given us the Bible, as **a manual of divine pedagogy,** reading which we sensitize and sharpen our inner ear to hear Her when She speaks today in the most unexpected moment, in the most unforeseen of circumstances and in the most unsuspected of places.[15]

3. Hebrew *dābār* and Greek *Logos*
God's Word cannot be circumscribed solely by the Greek *logos* which includes the meaning of **"idea"** (for *contemplating* the Creator and the creatures in the Creator — being an ingredient of traditional spirituality), and **"reason"** (for *explaining* the nature of creation and the Creator as

---

[15] See *Our Unhidden Agenda*, pp. 191-92.

37

happens in traditional theology).[16] This way of understanding 'spirituality' mainly as mystical contemplation and 'theology' mainly as a rational explanation has to be superseded in an Asian theology, which should rather re-appropriate **the notion of God's Word as God's *Will* implied in the Hebrew term *dābār*,** which denotes a "speech-request"; for in it we at once "hear" what is *spoken* and "obey" what is *requested*. That is why the biblical word for obedience is "hearing" (*šāma'*) in Hebrew and *hypakoē* in Greek). For what we hear is not just music for our personal enjoyment but *a mandate with a **promise** attached*. Hence our conclusion:-

An authentic theology interprets God's Word not as an object for contemplation (in spirituality) or a means of explanation (in theology) but as *a mission to be accomplished*, that is to say, as an executive Word that *solicits action*. Since Christ is God's creative or executive Word, to which our response is listening-obedience, we Christians are by vocations "Hearers of the Word" as Luther believed (already before he left the Roman communion), and therefore **doers** of *what Jesus did* as well as **doers** of what *Jesus bade us do*. Obedience is discipleship. The **promise** attached to the Word refers to the sacred covenant (a marriage promise) by which *God and we* bind ourselves to *mutual obedience* as I shall soon explain in no. 6 below (pp.46-50).

An **Asian theology**, therefore, is primarily a **praxis**, a way of life, a spirituality of **obedience** made in response to God's "Word-Request" heard in our own social context in the light

---

[16] From Heraclitus onwards the Greeks were entertaining this idea of *logos* in connection with the origin and existence of the world. Even the evangelist John who yields to the Greek notion seems to absorb into it the notion of 'wisdom', which is discussed below.

of the prayerful reading of the Bible. Praxis, let me repeat, is the first formulation of a theory. Hence in our Asian context *spirituality is not derived from a theology* as in the scholastic tradition; rather, *theology is derived from a spiritual praxis of obedience.* For a genuine theology, which is an *interpretation* of God's Word, presupposes a life lived in conformity with the divine summons. Hence I suggest that the Canon Cardijn's formula "see-judge-act" be replaced by "listen-act-see"! A theological *view* (seeing) is the fruit of *obedience* (hearing-acting). It was when Peter *heard* the Word which Jesus spoke ("cast the net...") and *acted* accordingly (obedience), that he *saw* who Jesus really was and who Peter really was ("depart from me, Lord, for I am a sinner"). Since God's will for us is Her Word, Jesus Christ, it is *following him* that constitutes *our salvation.* Similarly, the ancient saying "to know Christ in order to love Him and then follow Him" also reflects a wrong sequence! It is by following him in love that we come to know him. "*Come* [after me] *and* [then] *see*" (Jn 1:39)

To hear God's Word, i.e., recognize Her Voice, is what "discernment" means; to act accordingly is "obedience". Biblical spirituality consists of **discerning the Word** (= seeking the will of God) and **obeying** It. The virtue of obedience or the habitual "*listening* mode accompanied by *action*" is something that constant Scripture reading effects in us, and is known in Greek as *diakrisis* usually translated as "**discernment**". Hence we can say that the Bible is destined by God to make its attentive reader a "discerning person", *anthropos diakritikos,* to borrow a powerful expression from Greek Christianity. **Only a person who is in a "listening mode" or "discerning mood" can ideally become a theologian like Mary, because his or her task is to hear the Word, internalize It through obedient action and announce It (*interpreting* It) in the language and the cultural idiom of his or her contemporaries —an**

39

essentially Marian task as indicated above. If I may transfer Ignatius' visual idiom to the Bible's auditory idiom, it is a question of "*hearing* God's Word in all things and hearing all things as God's word". For "things" are also "words" (*dᵉbārîm*) in the Hebrew Bible, as explained above.

4. Biblical Wisdom as "Discerning Love"

One of the significant forms of theologizing that I learnt from the Hebrew Bible is recorded in its so-called **wisdom literature,** where, unlike in the rest of the Written Word, the focus is not God speaking in history. Here, the biblical authors have appropriated the *gnosis-oriented* literature of gentile religions prevalent in Egypt, Babylonia and Greece, in an attempt at what we would today call contextualization, without compromising the *agapeic* thrust of the Revelation specific to the Bible. This is, as I said, an excellent Asian example of interpretation or theologizing.

The saving word is *Fear of the Lord,* which is declared to be [the *beginning of*] *Wisdom* (Job 28:28; Ps 111:10; Prov. 1:7; 9:10; 31:30). The word "fear" does not denote "dread" but *reverential love* towards God, an awesome feeling of gratitude for what She has so generously shared with us in Her *history* entangled with ours, a history consisting of the ongoing creation, redemption and consummation which we are summoned to *remember* within Her *Eternal Now* at each celebration of the paschal mystery. It is almost an equivalent of a "worshipful attitude towards God".[17] In the ethical tradition of the Jews, the word "fear" is understood in two ways: first as *fear of retribution* and then as *reverential love* and according to one Rabbinic opinion wisdom begins with fear of retribution but this wisdom in its turn results in

---

[17] NRSV translation of Deut. 6:13 as cited in Lk 4:8 in *Harper Collins Study Bible,* 1993 uses "worship" to translate "fear" in Greek.

reverential love.[18] Thanks to this species of biblical literature, the Asian theologians can learn the art of interpreting the predominantly *gnostic* idiom of other Asian religions such as Buddhism, Jainism, Vedantic Hinduism and Daoism within the predominantly *agapeic* framework of the Christian Kerygma. For Asian Christians live and interact in a social context permeated by a sapiential brand of religiosity.

The gentile literature of the empires surrounding Israel reflected the political concerns of imperial rulers, for whom the "knowledge idiom" seems to have indicated the wavelength of the ruling elite in those pyramidically structured governmental organizations, and also revealed their solicitude for the *wise* management of worldly affairs. That species of knowledge did not *necessarily* give *absolute* priority to the concern for inter-human justice and to the needs of the oppressed. In the Bible, by contrast, the dominant theme is God's covenantal love (*ḥesed*) and loyalty (*'ĕmet*) which are inseparably connected with covenantal justice (*ṣᵉdāqāh*) and its concrete socio-legal expression (*mišpāṭ*). Pure Gnosticism, or "Knowledge without Love", risks being insensitive to social oppression whereas Biblical Wisdom which is "knowledge permeated by love" (an agapeic gnosis or a gnostic agape), there is no such danger. Thus in the Wisdom literature of the Bible, we meet an example of theologizing, i.e., a species of biblical *interpretation* of a particular non-biblical social context without compromising the fidelity to the Collective Memory of Israel's Primordial Experience which was the supreme expression of God's *love* and *justice* towards the oppressed slaves and towards their oppressors.

---

[18] A Cohen and A.J. Rosenberg, *Proverbs: Hebrew Text and English Translation with an Introduction and Commentary,* The Soncino Press, Jerusalem, New York, Revised Edition, 1985, p.3, note on verse 3.

41

Furthermore this Wisdom, as the Bible understands, is also *God's creative partner*, i.e., the Executive *Word* by which God created all things, and hence *ever available* in creation as well as in human history for those who seek Her. At the beginning was the Word, i.e., Wisdom or "knowledge penetrated by love". This seems to be what Johanine *logos* is made to convey. For both "revelation" (which generates **knowledge**) and "salvation" (which is generated by *love*) has met in Wisdom, which is the Word by which all things were/are created and redeemed; this Word, which is both revelation and salvation was made flesh *in* Jesus and *as* Jesus. This Word (*dābār*) is both revelatory speech and slavific command tied to a promise and eliciting from us a saving *wisdom,* i.e., a saving **knowledge** of God born of deeds of selfless **love.**

It is this same understanding of Wisdom that recurs in the church's traditional spiritual literature as *discreta caritas* or "discerning love", (i.e., a discernment or knowledge rooted in love). For as St Paul puts it, love (*agape*) has to increase more and more in our knowledge (*epignosis*) and insight (*aisthesis*) so that we may be helped to *discern what is best* (Phil. 1:9), that is, to discern what is best before God. Love which is self-transcending (or, to put it negatively, self-abnegating or selfless) prevents knowledge from being self-seeking so that one could *know* (i.e., discern) God's will (i.e., God's *dābār*) without misinterpreting it through self-interest (See Sp.Ex. 189). This is why the biblical Word (*dābār*) is identified with biblical Wisdom (*ḥokmāh*) —compare Baruch 3:38 with Jn 1:14; and this identification has resulted in a new interpretation and it is called **wisdom theology,** which the feminists have unearthed for us after many centuries of neglect. The presupposition is that only a symbiosis of gnosis and agape —with differing accentuation of the one or the other in various religions of Asia— constitutes "discerning love" (the medium of **salvific**

42

experience) as well as "wisdom theology" (the **salvific discourse** itself). In fact all contemporary religions in Asia, both Abrahamic and non-Abrahamic, have integrated both idioms —the former predominantly love-centered, and the latter predominantly knowledge-oriented but neither group neglecting the one or the other dimension.

Regrettably, the traditional theology which had absorbed Greek wisdom without filtering it through biblical love ended up in scholasticism, a species of Gnosticism:- a speculative theology that theorized on redemption without being itself at the service of redemption. I presume that the Jewish Rabbis might have noted this deviation already in the early centuries of Christianity, for we see that in the Babylonian Talmud they have warned the Jews against 'Greek Wisdom' (*hokma yevenit*).[19] St Basil, himself a Greek Father, warned the Christians against Greek contemplation (which replaces the auditory idiom with the visual). St Paul's expression *diakrisis* (discernment) is a **love-inspired** *recognition* **of God's Word;** for it is the "wisdom of the Cross" —the Cross being the supreme symbol of the highest Love. Such 'love-inspired knowledge of God' or wisdom, results in one's conformity with God's Word which is God's Salvific Will that expresses the path of liberation, both social and personal. The Asian theologian, therefore has to be a **discerning person** (*anthropos diakritikos*); only such a person can both *hear/obey* and *interpret* God's Word (both Scriptural and contemporary) for our times and for our people.

5. Mary: the Feminine Manifestation the Divine Word which is Wisdom.

The clash of views on the role of Mary, as entertained and defended by various denominations of Jesus-followers,

---

[19] Cf. Jonathan Sacks, *Future Tense, A Vision for Jews and Judaism in the Global Culture*, Hodder and Stoughton, London, 2009, p. 223. (**Hence forward** *Future Tense*)

constitute one of the divisive elements that have contributed to the evangelically counterproductive image of a *dismembered Body Christ* that the Christian churches project before the non-Christian majority in Asia. Ecumenicity is a missiological necessity in Asia. We cannot wait till the Western Churches, which imported these divisions, patch up their differences. The veneration and imitation of Mary need not be a source of dissension. The sober and sane Mariology such as upheld in the Oriental churches as well as the ecumenically accommodative theology of Mary worked out by the Roman Communion in *Lumen Gentium* of Vatican II and in *Marialis Cultus* of Paul VI is a healthy *via media* between the pre-Conciliar *Mariolatry* of a few conservative and retrogressive Catholics, on the one hand, and the *Mariophobia* of the so-called "free" Christian groups that operate in the remote fringes of Reformed Churches, on the other.

Ecumenically, therefore, Mariology has a strategic role to play in the churches of our continent where the association of the divine with the feminine is widely accepted phenomenon in many religions as evidenced in the popular cults of *Kāli, Dūrga, Pattini, Sarasvatī, Kuan Yin* (*Kanon*) and so on. For God's image is reflected in humanity's gender-duality (Gen. 1:27) and therefore the feminine dimension needs to complement the male image in any God-discourse besides needing to be reflected in *all* church ministries.

The feminist movement cutting across the churches *should help us all* to re-assess the role of Mary in the enfleshment, birth, growth, and presentation of the Word of God —in short her **Mothering the Divine,** as the evangelist declares in the words of Elizabeth: "the Mother of my Lord" (Lk 1:43). She began her earthly pilgrimage as the **"Virgin"**, i.e., a non-productive woman who, as such, was not adulated in Israel (unlike in pagan Greece and Rome known for parthenolatry

44

or virgin-cult); her virginity, therefore, symbolized evangelical poverty in that she boasts of her *non reliance on any human agency* ("I know not man"), and who, in other words relied solely on God ("Here I am your slave girl, let it be done according to Your Word"). Thus she became a **"Mother"** through *obedience to the Word*— which entitles her to be called the **"Disciple"** of Christ par excellence, the one who did "hear the word and keep it", and who followed the Word to the bitter end, thus   deserving the Johanine epithet of honour, **"Woman"** (Jn 2:4 and 19:26) because she pre-figured *The Woman* (Rev. 12:1; 17:31), the prototype of the redeemed humankind or the resurrected People of God constituting the Church of the Future. Mary, therefore, is the first member and the model of the church —the church, which therefore is called to imitate *her* in Christian discipleship.[20] She is also the model for theologians, who like her, are called to hear and receive the Word, ponder over it in their hearts, assist Its growth and release it to the Faithful. The church should never forget that *its first Minister of The Word was a woman.*

This theological reflection led me to see Mary as *Prajñā Pīṭha,* a literal translation of "Seat of Wisdom" of the traditional Marian Litany; it can also be rendered into English as the *Chair of Philosophy,*[21] or (in the vocabulary of St John Damascene who defined theology as wisdom) the *Chair of Theology* but signifying metaphorically, the one who **bears the Word which is Wisdom** —*bears* both in the sense of

---

[20] How this Marian role is crystallized in the two Marian dogmas (Immaculate Conception and Assumption, not accepted in reformed churches) is discussed in *Give Vatican II a Chance: Yes to Incessant Renewal, No to Reform of the Reforms,* Kelaniya, 2010, pp. 121-122. With Rahner and many other theologians, we too would do well to distinguish between central and peripheral dogmas in the Roman Communion and leave these two Marian dogmas in the latter category for ecumenical reasons.

[21] Originally I coined the term *Prajñā Pīṭha* as the official name of the Faculty of Philosophy of our Jesuit Province.

45

"birthing" as a mother and in the sense of "holding" as a seat or a chair does. In the Indic cultures such a person is recognized in *Sarasvatī*, the goddess of art, wisdom and culture who is always depicted with the Vīnā, a Lamp and a book containing the Word, and aptly referred to as *Vāgdevī* the **feminine manifestation of the divine Word.**[22] This Marian epithet serves as the title of a Theological Journal I edit and has been immortalized in a sculpture that graces the premises of our Tulana Centre (pp.136-137).

6. Obedience to the Word: Never Blind but *Dialogical* and *Reciprocal,*

The foundation of our Faith is *the Covenant* which God of Moses and Jesus has sealed with *all* persons of all places and times, both those who have <u>chosen to be poor</u> *for the sake of God's Reign* and others who are <u>forced to be poor</u> *by the beneficiaries of Mammon's Reign.* God promises that if we observe our part of the covenant stipulations, then the second category of the poor would be eliminated (Dt. 15:4-6). Since this covenant is enfleshed in and as Jesus-Christ, the Christians among the covenant-partners (i.e. among the world's poor) are super-eminently called to publicly profess their fidelity to the terms of the treaty. Furthermore, this covenant is not an unequal contract between a powerful monarch and powerless subjects or a business agreement between a merchant and his clients; rather, it is *an understanding between two parties in love* —the implication being that there is a *parity of status* between God and us. For love is an equalizer. Hence all negotiations pertaining to the Covenant between God and us demand *dialogue* and *reciprocity.* The consequence of this glorious arrangement is awesome:- **God and we** <u>**dialogue**</u> **with each other before**

---

[22] See "Prajñā Pītha: "Seat of Wisdom": Towards a Marian Formation of the Ministers of the Word", *VJTR*, 63/1, January 1999, 7-20 (Part One), 63/2, February 1999, 103-118 (Part Two); *EAPR*,35/2 1998, 167-200.

we obey each other! Both parties are bound by a mutual obedience which is preceded by a frank dialogue.

(a) DIALOGICAL OBEDIENCE.
Before giving her word of obedience in response to God's word-request, Mary questioned God about the 'how' of the Saviour's conception, declaring her own stance with regard to the possibility of conceiving him. Such a dialogue was not a breach of faith as it seemed in the case of Zacharias. It was her faith in God that made her feel so free as to clarify matters before giving her consent. The Old Testament bears witness to a more radical form of this approach to God's Words or speech-commands. As Rabbi Jonathan Sachs has put it:

> Judaism is about conversation. It is the only religion known to me in which human beings talk to, argue and remonstrate with God. Abraham argues with God. So do Moses, Jeremiah, Jonah and Job. There is nothing remotely like this in the sacred books of either Christianity or Islam.[23]

Mary's example and the Syro-Phenician woman's retorts to Jesus' harsh remarks, *pace* Sachs, are vestiges of the Jewish tradition contained in the New Testament. Hence we Christian should not lose sight of our Jewish heritage; for according to the Jewish Law, even if the Sanhedrin members are unanimous in finding a person guilty of a capital offense, its verdict is null and void unless they have a trial in which both sides are heard. In fact Nicodemus (Nakdimon) refers to this law in his defense of Jesus: "Our Torah doesn't condemn a man —does it?— until after hearing from him and finding

---

[23] *Future Tense,* p.183.

47

out what he is doing" (Jn 7:51).[24] Rabbi Sacks explains how
God follows this policy:-

> In the case of God, we have faith in the total justice
> of his decree. But in Judaism faith is not blind.
> Therefore there must be a trial, that is what the
> dialogue between Abraham and God is. The
> plaintiff is God, representing justice. The accused
> are the people of Sodom. Abraham is cast by God
> in the role of a counsel for defense. The Judge of
> all the earth cannot be seen to be performing justice
> until the case for the defense has been made.[25]

This is what obedience (*hypakoē*) means in the Bible. But
early Christianity, drifting away from its Collective Memory,
had introduced an anti-scriptural model of obedience
(*hypotagē*), namely a blind submission to the will of a human
superior who claims to be standing and speaking for God —
a god of gentiles, of course, not the God of the Covenanted
People. Christian obedience ought to be directed only to God,
and never to a human being (Acts 5:29). Both in the Church
and in some religious congregations it is the pagan *hypothagē*
and not the biblical *hypakoē* that is practised. A Christian
cannot be silenced without a hearing, without a friendly but
frank dialogue. Our ways of government today do not often
tally with God's ways.

Ignatian obedience, misconstrued as a blind execution of a
military command, is so close to the scriptural *hypakoē* that
the church authorities would do well to study it as a model in
handling those Christians, specially the creative thinkers
whom they too easily label and even censure as deviants. For
Ignatius never advocated a blind obedience to a superior;

---

[24] Translation from the *Jewish New Testament*, (tr. David H.Stein), Jewish New
Testament Publications, Jerusalem, Maryland, USA, 1989, p.130.
[25] *Future Tense*, p. 195.

rather the superior and his or her *companion* (misconceived as a "subject") are both called to **seek God's will** *together* through prayerful dialogue with God and with each other and thus **obey God** *together*. In the scandalously inhuman treatment of Tissa Balasuriya, there was no proper dialogue but a unilateral command to agree to a theologically erroneous statement authored by a local bishop and an illicit profession of faith imposed upon him by a Roman authority under pain of automatic excommunication. It was an inhuman approach as anti-biblical as it was anti-canonical.[26] Our highest authorities in the church must be persuaded to return to the *Sources* as Vatican II has requested and act according to the mind of YHWH, the God of Moses and Jesus.

(b) RECIPROCAL OBEDIENCE.

Biblical obedience is not only dialogical but eminently *reciprocal*. It is not only God who says "*Hear* me O Israel" (i.e. obey Me) but it is equally *our* right to repeat the same speech-command to God, "*Hear* us O Lord" (do what we ask you). This **mutual obedience** is one of the stipulation of our Covenant with our maternal Father. The Covenant is an agreement between partners in love —love which makes the partners equal. If we are faithful to the covenant, as God certainly is, then we share with God the right to be mutually heard i.e., mutually obeyed! Just as Her Word is a speech-command, so would ours be —if only we are *faith-ful* to our divine Partner, i.e., *full of faith* in Her. If the small amount of faith (*metron pisteos*), which is all that is infused into us (Rom. 12:3) does not remain "little faith", which Jesus repudiates (Mt 6:30; 8:26; 14:31; Mk 4:40; Lk 12:28; 8:25) but grows, "like a mustard seed" into a "great faith" which Jesus admires and recommends (Mt 8:10; 15:28;Lk 7:9), then

---

[26] See "The Balasuriya Affair: A Healthy Crisis in an Island Church", Lieve Troch (ed.) *Rainbows on a Crying Planet*, Tiruvalla, India, 2003, pp. 185-204.

we simply utter the word " move!" and the mountain moves, as Jesus has assured us (Mt 17:20) . *Our* word becomes God's speech-command. For our faith in God is God's omnipotence operating within us. It is our constant obedience to God's Word that helps us to "increase our faith" to such magnitude as to turn "our prayers into executive-words![27]

To cite one among many examples, Elijah the Prophet *obeyed* the Word of God each time he heard it and God *obeyed* Elijah's word with equal promptness and fidelity! Seeing which, the Widow exclaimed "Now I know that you are a man of God and that the Word of the Lord in your mouth is the truth" (I K Ch 17:24), The authority (another name for 'credibility') of a theologian lies in the occurrence, in his or her life, of this *reciprocal obedience* so that the Word he *interprets* is accepted as "Truth" (which in, the Hebrew text, is *'ĕmet,* God's *being true to* Her Word or fidelity to the covenant). Our great Asian spiritual masters even of other religions did not have recourse to copious footnotes to affirm their authority, which sprang from their personal witness rather than from the confirmation of others.

7. "Faith" and "Good Works" in Asian Liberation Theology

The *common platform*, on which *both* the Romans and the Lutherans of the 16th century were standing when they were debating 'for and against' *sola fides,* was a very *shaky* theology of redemption —a theology based on a purely juridical view of sin, expressed in terms of guilt, judgment and punishment and couched in the Roman jurisprudential language. Perhaps it was Augustinianism that clouded the issue. Thus some Christians of the later generations of both parties ended up advocating a blasphemous theory of atonement in which a revengeful God is believed to have imposed on the divine Son a cruel death penalty meant to

---

[27] See *Our Unhidden Agenda,* p. 109.

satisfy the divine wrath against humankind and thus remove its guilt.[28] But according to our Collective Memory, the fruit of sin is not so much 'guilt' as eternal *death*; and that salvation is brought about not by punishment but by the restoration of *life*, which the dead cannot do for themselves but is the gracious initiative of a merciful God; but the redemptive process, which only begins with this divine initiative cannot continue without our cooperation in the *healing* and the *nourishing* of our resuscitated lives. As members of a covenant we too have a role to play in our own redemption. This biblico-patristic paradigm (or something close to it) is reported to have been advocated by the sole surviving representatives of the Antiochean school of theology participating in the Council of Trent —only to be shouted down by the scholastics who had accused them of crypto-Protestantism.[29]

Since Liberation Theology in Asia is stamped by and built on the spiritual praxis of *obedience to the Word of God*, the aforementioned debate between the Romans and Reformers has been laid to rest and has ceased to be an issue in the mainline churches, at least in our country, thanks to what we describe below (pp.109-111) as "trans-ecclesial ecumenism". As I have argued elsewhere on the solid basis of our Collective Memory,[30] Roman Catholics can and should whole-heartedly agree with what Luther (as well as St Thomas Aquinas three centuries before Luther) had declared:- *"sola fide"* (salvation by faith alone) — but not without adding that faith is neither an intellectual assent to a

---

[28] I have supplied examples in "What on Earth is God Doing with Us? A Search for Authentic Christian Theism", *Gleanings,* (Ecumenical Institute, Colombo) January-June 2008, pp.3-16 **(Hence forward *Gleanings*)**

[29] Cf. Barry Collett, *Italian Benedictine Scholars and the Reformation,* Oxford, 1985, Chapters 4-8; also "Benedictine Origins of a Mid-Sixteenth Century Heresy, *The Journal of Religious History,* June 1986, p. 17ff.

[30] *Our Unhidden Agenda,* Ch. II; see also "Dogmas, Faith and God's Word: Eleven Irksome Questions for the 'Year of Faith' (2012)", *Vagdevi,* 12 (July 2012), 41-65.

propositional truth found in the Scriptures or in church teachings (as *some* Roman Catholics think), nor a mere verbal confession of accepting Jesus as one's savior (as some evangelical protestants believe). Rather, faith (*ĕmûnāh*) which means 'reliance' or 'trust') in the One who is faithful ('*ĕmet* which means 'reliable' or 'trustworthy') is experienced through *obedience* (listening followed by *action*) to that Trustworthy One's Word, which is a *speech-command* with the *promise* of salvation attached to it. That is why James tells us that Abraham's justification by faith refers to his *obedience in executing God's command*, that is, his *action* of offering his son back to God (Ja 2:21-24) in compliance with God's Word; righteousness was not credited to him for works of the law such as ritual sacrifices or circumcision, but for obedient action. Underline <u>action</u>.

There are two parables in which Jesus seems to tell us that even the *non-believers* can attain eternal life provided they demonstrate their love for their neighbors through an appropriate *action*. Love, which alone is eternal (I Cor 13:8) and is greater than faith (I Cor 13:2c) is expected of all people, even of those who do not profess faith in the God of Moses and Jesus. It is the *universal* means of salvation in the dispensation of Jesus. In the parable of the Good Samaritan, two 'believers' in YHWH are prevented by their own adherence to the Law [of purity] from *acting* as a neighbor towards a victim of robbery and violence, whereas the Samaritan, despite being branded as someone who had abandoned his faith in YHWH, *does* the needful at great cost to himself and is therefore recommended by Jesus as the one who fulfilled the requirement for gaining eternal life; "go and *do* as he *did*", Jesus said to the Teacher of the Law (Lk 10:25-37). In the parable of the Last Judgment, Jesus reveals that even the "Nations" (*gôyim*) —who presumably are not a "People" *('am)* that recognize YHWH or pray to Her or publicly profess their *faith* in Her— enter eternal life on the

52

basis of their *works* of love and justice on behalf of those deprived of basic needs and freedoms (Mt 25: 31-46). From the non-believing nations (including atheists) the God of Moses and Jesus expects **works of love and justice** as the absolute condition for attaining salvation!

The intimate nexus between *faith* and *justice*[31] as revealed to us by the prophets including Jesus implies that idolatry or greed, which is the opposite of *faith* (Prov.28:25), is associated with the opposite of *justice* (i.e., injustice). Hence the authentic **worship** of God (which is an expression of our faith) and **inaction** in the face of injustice are **incompatible**. Those, therefore, who dare to love enough to engage themselves in works of justice are cryptic *believers in* and anonymous *worshipers of* the One who judges nations according to the criterion: "Whatever you *do* to the least of my brothers and sisters you *do* it to Me" (Mt 25:40). For salvation is promised to the "doers" of God's will, not to those who say "Lord, Lord" (Mt 7:21).

Hence in Asia, the Liberation Theologians are *ecumenically* united in upholding that salvation is offered not on the basis of "works of the law" such as the performance of rites and rituals, organizing prayer rallies and open-air masses, paying tithes and mass-stipends, but on *'ābad* (Hebrew for "work"), which also expresses the notion of "service" rendered to one's neighbor and over nature (cf. *'ābad* in Gen.2:5;15) as well as "service" (meaning "worship") rendered unto God.[32] Mutual *Service* (or volunteering to work as servants of one another) is apiece with the act of Eucharistic *Worship* (Cf. Jn 13: 4-14).[33] It is with this Scripture-based understanding of faith vis-à-vis love —love which alone saves and is

---

[31] *Our Unhidden Agenda*, chapter II
[32] Explained in detail in *Mysticism of Service*, (Tulana, Kelaniya, 2000) pp. 79-83 and in *Our Unhidden Agenda*, pp. 52-54.
[33] *Our Unhidden Agenda*, 52-54.

expressed in our service to others— that we Christians from many denominations, partnered, of course, by the God of Exodus and Resurrection, work together with other religionists and even with non-religionists for the *liberation* of both the oppressed and their oppressors.

8. Summary and Conclusion

The Bible, as we have explained, is not only a book revealing God's Word which is Creative Wisdom personified in Jesus the Christ, but is equally a book of *many interpretations* of that Word and, therefore, a book containing *many theologies!* Reading it we learn how the inspired writers themselves had re-interpreted past slavific events according to *the new* social contexts which at times included the judicious appropriation of doctrines and the literature of *other religions.* Thus the same event could be seen to be interpreted in different and even opposing ways in response to the salvific needs of changed circumstances. By providing many models of theology, the Bible also *educates us to theologize* and also to accept pluralism in theology.

The manner in which Israel recognized God in its own 'history', as revealed to us when reading the Bible, is how we are called to interpret our own history as a locus of divine interventions. For history is not chronology, a mere record of events. History is a particular way of seeing events and even *restructuring* them along a particular perspective. *This perspective is God and God's liberative intervention in these events, specially on behalf of Her covenant partners, the slaves of all times and places.* To understand those biblical theologies, which interpret and rearrange ancient happenings according to the redemptive presence and redemptive activity of God in every new life-situation, we have to master the **socio-historical circumstances** that led these sacred authors to *interpret* God's Word *for their times and for their people.* Such a background knowledge of the history and culture of

Israel and its neighbours is a must in the training programme of a *formal* theologian.

Hence it goes without saying that a theologian has to be equipped with two kinds of tools: (a) **the tools of biblical exegesis** *to comprehend the Word in Scriptures in accordance with varying contexts* (see Chapter VI for an Asian approach to exegesis); and (b) **tools of socio-historical analysis** *to grasp our own contemporary situation* (Asian as well as global) in which the same divine Word is heard. The formation of an Asian theologian must necessarily include these two kinds of training, without neglecting, however, the contribution of other Asian religions, specially gnosis-centred ones which offer us valuable **tools of self-analysis.** For there cannot be two divine voices, one heard in the Bible and another in contemporary history; their coincidence has to be recognized by every Christian, and *a fortiori* by the formal theologian. This is where many theologies and theologians *could* fail were they to go along a mere "explanatory" approach based on the Greek *logos* as the Rational Idea, rather than along *a praxis of loving obedience* here and now to the Hebrew *dābār*, God's Redemptive Will, Her Liberating Word of Wisdom soliciting action.

Which means, theology has to be Mary's *fides sperans salutem,* "faith that aspires for liberation" as I have argued on the basis of *Lumen Gentium* elsewhere.[34] Since liberation *(salus)* in biblical revelation is *love* which alone is redemptive, it follows that theology is also *fides respirans amorem,* "faith that breathes love". For love is the faith that drives us to live and die for others (Cf. Gal 5:6). A theology that does not encourage such faith is as sterile as *fides*

---

[34] Aloysius Pieris, "Christ Beyond Dogma: Doing Christology in the Context of the Religions and the Poor," *Louvain Studies* (Catholic University of Leuven), 25 (2000): p.197 ff. **(Hence forward "Christ Beyond Dogma")**

quaerens intellectum ("faith seeking understanding"), a notion of theology that epitomizes the methodology of the Christological councils which, though eminently correct in what they said, had regrettably ignored soteriology (**love** revealed by the crucified Christ) due to their excessive preoccupation with gnosis —a mere **knowledge** of *how* the divine *logos* had assumed 'human nature' rather than an "interior relishing" (*res interne gustare*) of the mystery of God's *dābār* becoming *bāśār* (God's *Rhema* becoming *sarx*), i.e., the awesome revelation that Eternal Word became *vulnerable* or *fleshy* like us humans and experienced pain and death out of that love which saved us! Though these councils were dominated by bishops from the *Eastern* Churches, their thinking was saturated with the Greek philosophical idiom, somewhat like the typically *Western theology* created by the *African theologian* Augustine, who thought and wrote in Latin, the language of the Roman colonizer! An Asian theology has to be rooted in the biblical writings and thought out in Asian languages rather than in the languages of the foreign rulers.[35][]

---

[35] See the prolonged exchange of arguments that Norman Tanner and I shared on this issue in *VJTR*, 67 (September 2003), pp. 782-92, and in the ensuing discussion between us: his response in *VJTR*, 67 (November 2003), pp. 948-54; my reflection on his response in *VJTR*, 68 (April 2004), p. 301; his counter-reply in *VJTR*, 68 (April 2004), pp. 302-4; and my concluding comment in *VJTR*, 68 (September 2004), pp. 702-3.

Part Two

A Personal Search for the Method

CHAPTER III
The Primordial Experience and the Collective Memory
MY ATTEMPT TO EXPERIENCE, UNDERSTAND AND INTERPRET THEM WITHIN THE ASIAN CONTEXT

Let me begin with a confession. My first ten or twelve years of Religious Life were a restless period of search. Things did not hold together. My mind and heart, my knowledge and love, my prayer and action, my love for God and love for neighbour were running on parallel lines. The integration came only after Vatican II and GC 31 (the 31st General Congregation of the Jesuits). In these two events —the church in the former and the Jesuits in the latter— rediscovered their *origins* and recovered their *primordial* insights. With that renewal, things began to fall into place. This was the beginning of an action-filled reflection that I transposed into a theology in the 1970s in the company of many other Asians. In this process we, from different parts of Asia, were passing through a long process of learning, which began with initial *conversations* that led to several *controversies* and ended in eventual *convergences*. I recount this rather *long* story in this chapter and in the next.

1. Biblical Framework: History, not Philosophy
The Spirit of Vatican II stormed into our Pontifical Faculty of Theology in Naples where my studies coincided with the four

years of the Council. The reliable framework for theologizing was no more a "rational system" such as Aristotelian philosophy but *history* understood in the peculiarly biblical sense. This shift was the fruit of decades of spade-work done by Catholic scripture scholars initially led by the Protestant colleagues. There seemed to be a general consensus in our Faculty about the need to return to the sources of Christianity, specially Scriptures where the *God of History* had revealed Herself to all the people of the world through the *Story* of one People *chosen* for that purpose.

Providentially I had already taken a rather strange decision, at the age of about sixteen, to stop reading novels and take to reading history as a pastime! What whetted my appetite for this new hobby were a few entertainingly written books on the history of Western music and musicians freely available in the common Reading Room of the Jesuits' St Aloysius, College (Galle) where I completed my secondary education. While preparing for my GCE 'A' Level (as an external student of the London University) at the age of 18 plus, the prescribed syllabus for Pali language made me delve into Indian History from Mohenjadaro to the Mogul period. I enjoyed it so much that I passed with distinction in that subject! After I had entered the Jesuit Philosophate —for I was exempted from the usual two year training period known as the Juniorate[36] — I had devoured several tomes on the history of both Western and Indic philosophy.

---

[36] Such exemptions are a privilege given only to late-vocations but I was only 21 years when the superiors decided that my knowledge of Greek and Latin (taught in the Juniorate) was more than sufficient to continue my philosophical and theological studies immediately after the Novitiate! Already as a novice I was asked to follow the regular courses in Greek in the Juniorate so that at the end of my Novitiate I was ready for Philosophy! As for Latin, I had been privileged to begin the study of that language at the age of twelve under Fr Michael de Give, s.j., —my spiritual guide since that tender age and Professor of Greek and Latin at the Papal Seminary (which was walking distance from my house), who guided me into the Society of Jesus but is a Cistercian Monk today, still inspiring and guiding me from a distance— so that by fourteen I was reading both the New Testament and the *Imitatio Christi* in

Thanks to the far-sightedness of Fr de Rotton, our Rector at Sacred Heart College (our Philosophate) at Shembaganur, India, we were made to attend the famous Austrian Jesuit Hoffinger's inspiring talks on "the Catechetical Value of the Liturgy." That was in the mid-1950s, a few years before Vatican II. At that time, as the Choir Director, I was blindly following the pre-Vatican II tradition of entertaining a liturgically passive congregation with a polyphonic concert every Sunday and Feast Day! Hoffinger awakened us to the true nature of worship and the active participatory role of the People of God in it as well as its pedagogical potentialities, not to mention the theological necessity of worshipping in one's own native language! He unfolded the *history* of both liturgy and spirituality from the earliest times to instill in us the desire to renew our collective worship according to the authentic but neglected tradition. Since then, beginning with my regency-cum-study period that followed immediately i.e., (1959-1962 in Sri Lanka), I made use of my free time and, of course, the holidays to read and assimilate whatever I could grab on the *history* of Liturgy and *history* of Spirituality available in our Libraries.

In fact by the time I started theology in Naples in 1962, I had read quite a few classics on Liturgy authored by such writers as Jungmann, Parsch, Brasso *et al.* During theological studies in Naples, I enjoyed perusing Righetti's voluminous work, *La Storia della Liturgia.* In fact my STL thesis was a *historical study* of the role of Scripture in the Latin Liturgy. My Rectors (Gustavo Galeota and his successor, Francesco Bruno) were

---

Latin and later obtained distinction in that subject at O'Level examination. Thus in the Novitiate, I was assigned to teach Latin to the other novices and was asked to follow the advanced Juniorate students' class in which they were reading Augustine in Latin under the Latinist , Fr Pullen! This explains the unusual exemption from the Juniorate, normally restricted to those who join late in life!!!! To reduce two years from the long formation period of a Jesuit was a boon in deed!

so generous as to allow me to follow courses and seminars in various parts of Italy conducted by eminent *periti* who drafted Vatican II's *Sacrosanctum Concilium* such as Salvatore Marsili, Hermann Schmidt and so on and I also sought the advice of Cipriano Vagaggini in writing my thesis. The history of liturgy led me to the history of the church and history of theology! After my theology I continued my interest in other areas like history of art and architecture, history of various forms of Asian Buddhism and so on. I found history more engaging than fiction! *History, History, History, History!* This was the refrain I heard and, therefore, the one that I hummed to myself ever since... and still sing for all to hear in season and out of season. As for the notion of history which I had in mind when reading the Scriptures, I prefer to discuss it Chapter V (pp.143-144).

Until I started theological studies I thought, quite foolishly, of course, that what had prepared me for the study of theology was my presumed mastery of "scholastic philosophy" —on which I wrote seven hand-written manuals in Latin, believing it to be the *philosophia perennis* which I would "teach all nations" one day! Three of these seven manuals have survived the ravages of time and are safely deposited in our Tulana Library as three archaeological pieces! But it was at the very inception of my theological studies that it dawned on me how Providence had prepared me for the study of the Sacred Scriptures by instilling in me since youth a fascination for history, though I do not regret the time and the energy spent on Aristotle and specially on Thomas, whom I still treasure as a razor-sharp analyst (able to split a question into several of them!) and whose *Summa* I frequently consult.

During my theological studies, I sought the Rector Gustavo Galeota's permission, which was readily granted, to study the OT in Hebrew under the *personal* guidance of the renowned scripture scholar Stefan Porubçan, formerly of Rome's *Biblicum*. He was a colossal failure in the lecture hall but a stupendous success as a personal tutor in his private chamber. I was fascinated by the biblical world, the Semitic or early West Asian mentality of the biblical authors, the plastic this-worldly idiom and the symbolic texture of their discourse. Thus the *History of Israel* (history as an interpreted arrangement of orally transmitted events) became another area of interest. The anthropology and the cosmology of the Bible seemed more down-to-earth and liberating than Aristotelo-Thomism. Hence under the influence of the new ecclesial climate that dawned during the Second Vatican Council, I was made to confront the scholastic theology built on philosophy with the soteriology transmitted in the typically Hebrew idiom that is characteristic not only of the "history" unfurled in the OT but also in the Semitic mind-set hiding behind the Greek texts of the NT.

My professor, Stefan Proubçan was so happy with my study of Hebrew and the OT that he gifted me his own personal copy of the Hebrew OT (with his name written on it in his own handwriting and now conserved, here, in our Tulana Library) making me promise that I would use it for my *daily* spiritual reading. (I still read my psalms in Hebrew with the official text that the Jews use today). Later I met Stanislaus Lyonnet another great scripture scholar at Rome's *Biblicum* and sought to be guided by him personally in my early search for an "Asian theology unencumbered by Greek Philosophy". I looked for a Western Biblical scholar critical of the West's *post-Thomistic scholastic theology*. And he was my find, though a true Thomist himself. Thus the need to consult the *collective memory* (or "scripture and tradition" according to the older vocabulary) became almost an obsession for me.

2. "Mystical Contemplation" and the Primordial Experience

The problem I had with scholastic theology after the encounter with the Hebrew Scriptures also troubled me when I started questioning the kind of 'spiritual experience' that the Ignatian Exercises have been mediating for me during the first decade of my Jesuit life. Jan Philipp Roothaan's excessively rational excursus on Ignatian meditation, recommended to us in the nineteen fifties, did not resonate with what I was searching for. Fortunately, this was also the time when half a century of research into Ignatian sources had brought out the affinity of the early Jesuit spirituality with the Bible's *mysticism of service*. The 31st General Congregation of the Jesuits (GC 31) was also taking place during the Council (i.e., during my theological studies) and things began to make sense. I started re-experiencing Christ of the Ignatian Exercises in the light of the *Creative Word* heard within the Bible and without. The Exodus-Resurrection of the Judeo-Christian tradition (*primordial experience*) began to dominate my personal retreats as the *id quod volo* ("that which I want"), to borrow an Ignatian idiom. This Biblico-Ignatian synthesis which I strove to internalize is amply demonstrated in the articles I have published on spirituality from 1979 onwards —now assembled to form my 13th book.[37] My Ignatian praxis of Scriptural soteriology was inseparable from my reading of God's Word in the context of Asian/Sri Lankan history. Here I followed almost literally the exhortation given in Vatican II that we Religious should renew ourselves by going back not only to the charism of our founders but also to the [written and unwritten] sources of Christianity (*Perfectae Caritatis*, no 2).

From about the 17th century onwards, the primordial salvific experience of Christianity (or "liberational spirituality") had

---

[37] *Our Unhidden Agenda: How We Jesuits Work, Pray and Form Our Men* (Kelaniya, 2012).

been identified with what is normally referred to as "mystical contemplation", a sort of one-to-one encounter in which the human person is absorbed into an ecstatic divine embrace.[38] It is sometimes referred to as the "immediate experience of God", though one wonders whether there could be any human experience that is not mediated. I also realized that the whole discourse on "ascetical and mystical theology" consists of an *interpretation of a type of prayer*, which begins with active engagement with God in a one-to-one conversation ("ascetical stage") and ends up with an allegedly passive absorption into Her divine Self ("mystical state").

Being an *interpretation* it needs to be tested against the biblical Christianity's collective memory, which clearly points to the fact that all the saints of the OT as well as Christ's holy followers mentioned in the NT have never been called into an intimacy with God as an end in itself, but always as a prelude to a *mission,* to which they are sent and accomplishing which they found their salvation. I am *called* to be with God only to be *sent* on an errand which determines my final redemption. For God's Word that *calls* us is always a command to *do* something for the coming of Her Reign, like the Twelve whom Jesus "appointed *to be with him* and *to be sent out*" (Mk 3:14. Italics added). **Being with Jesus** ["in the days of his flesh"] did not last more than three years for them but their mission continued for decades preaching the good news that Christ ["as we know him now"] is available in the least of his brothers and sisters, and that "nations" who do not 'know" Jesus can still meet, serve and **be with** him in **the needy** (Mt 25: 31-46).

---

[38] Critically assessed in *God's Reign for God's Poor, : A Return to the Jesus Formula,* (Tulana, Kelaniya, 1999) pp. 10-18. **(Hence forward God's Reign for God's Poor)**

It is against the background of these reflections that I searched for the exact place that the *individual* mystical experiences occupy in the spiritual landscape of *biblical* Christianity. Who came to my rescue? **Teresa of Avila**, the great Doctor of Spiritual Theology and a 'contemplative' par excellence. In her *Interior Castle,* she clearly affirms that such prayer-experiences do not constitute "union with the will of God" (her term for spirituality or experience of salvation); rather, what ensures that experience, she avers emphatically, is one's loving service to the needy neighbor, even within the cloister.[39]

Here she is scriptural to the core. For according to the NT, love of neighbor expressed in selfless service fulfils the law and the prophets (Mt 7:12), that is to say, love of neighbour is the sum and substance of revelation and salvation. This is a recurrent theme in the New testament (Rom 13:8-10; Gal 5:14; Jas 2:8;Jn 13:34; 14:15; 15:12, 17). Mystical contemplation is a charisma, a gift and is therefore meant for *others,* i.e., to build up the community, and not necessarily a sure guarantee of one's own salvation; on the contrary such gifts can be misused for self-aggrandizement. For I believe that God does not call someone to such intimacy without a mission in view as we have already averred in the light of our collective memory (scriptures etc); which means that the mission of contemplatives cannot be identified with mystical prayer as such but with the *service* they render to the whole church *as its incessant intercessors.* The *mission* to which they are *called* is to pray for the world and the church, as did Abraham, Moses and other patriarchs and also prophets of Israel, not to mention Jesus.[40]

---

[39] In *Our Unhidden Agenda,* Chapter VI, I discuss this issue at greater length, citing the relevant text from Teresa's *Interior Castle.*
[40] "A Priest-Uncle's Letter to a Niece on the Day She Entered the Great Carmel", *The Missionary Oblate,* (De Mazenod House, Colombo) 10, July-December 1994, pp. 2-6.

It is true that both **Benedict and Ignatius**, two giants who gifted the church with a Scriptural spirituality, are each reported to have had an extraordinary encounter with the Divine, and that their experience would easily be categorized as a "mystical" experience. Significantly they are each reported by a third person: the former by St Gregory the Great in his *Dialogues*, and the latter by Luis Gonsalvez da Camara. It is a gift bestowed by God gratuitously in view of a mission, and to be accepted with humility. Presumably both saints were aware that divine visitations (that go by the name of mystical contemplation today) do not necessarily constitute the primordial experience of salvation. For their understanding of spirituality was based on other criteria. Hence the following observation:-

In the *Rule of Benedict* the word "contemplation" of Hellenistic provenance is conspicuously absent. What pervades the *Regula Benedicti* is the biblical spirituality of "listening": *our listening to God's Word* in the Scriptures as well as *God listening to our words* in the recitation of psalms and other prayers. Ignatius, too, would have us welcome mystical gifts but defined spirituality in terms of what we might call a **continuous "listening mode"**; i.e. a habitual openness to God's summons which presupposes a detachment from one's own self (Sp.Ex, no 23, 89); a sort of perpetual proneness to *discern* God's Will and *execute* it. It is a spirituality of *obedience,* namely, an uninterrupted attitude of *listening to and acting on God's speech-commands.* It is this incessant God-awareness or mindfulness of God that Jeronimo Nadal, one of the first Fathers of the Society of Jesus, meant when he coined the much misunderstood expression *contemplativus simul ac in actione* ("contemplative even in action"). It is an activist's spirituality of continuous prayerfulness even amidst action, a *mysticism* *of service* and not an alternation between mystical contemplation and apostolic engagement![41]

Hence the tendency to equate "spirituality" with *mystical contemplation* of God and relegating *action* on behalf of one's neighbor to an holy extra is a heresy; it is not to be identified with the reliving of the primordial experience nor is it so recognized in our Collective Memory. Regrettably from early times Mary and Martha had come to symbolize the allegedly superior option for the contemplative life and the allegedly 'inferior' status of the active life, respectively![42] This interpretation goes against the fact that the notion and the term 'contemplation' (*theoria*) is conspicuously absent in the NT and even in the early Christian literature. In fact, what Jesus disapproved in Martha was not her service (*diakonia*) as such but that she was distracted (*periespato*) by her work, and unable to listen to the Word that Mary was listening to. Distraction, as Jesus insinuates in that same text, is accompanied by "anxiety" and "disturbance" of mind. Being ever mindful of God's Word or ever maintaining oneself in a listening mood in the midst of service and action without being "distracted" is the spirituality of obedience required of Jesus-follower. As mentioned above, biblical spirituality is one of *remembrance*, of being *ever mindful* of God, and of course being mindful of the poor, as I have argued in my study on Mindfulness.[43]

Our contention is that the primordial experience of liberation is available in the **encounter with the Risen Lord** who meets us in the guise of very ordinary people —e.g., the

[41] As explained at length in *Mysticism of Service : A Short Treatise on Spirituality with a Pauline-Ignatian Focus on the Prayer Life of Christian Activists*, Tulana Jubilee Publications, Kelaniya, 2000 **(Hence forward *Mysticism of Service*)**
[42] For a criticism of this interpretation and for further elucidation of the text, cf. *God's Reign for God's Poor*, p.17.
[43] "The Spirituality of Mindfulness: Biblical and Buddhist Approaches: *Spiritus*, 10 (2010), 38-51. Reprint in *Our Unhidden Agenda*, Ch. VIII.

gardener who meets Mary (Jn 20:15-16), the *stranger* who intrudes into our company (Lk 24: 13-35) or the *cook* who prepares our breakfast (Jn 21:9-12), and of course the neediest of neighbours (Mt 25: 31-46). To **heroically** *love my friends* by sacrificing for them my possessions including my own very life when necessary and to **forgivingly** *love my enemies* by completely erasing from my memory the evil they have done to me are the two inseparable dimensions of the **New Commandment** which Jesus proclaimed from the Cross, *by dying for us* and by *forgiving his enemies.* **Prayer** of whatever kind —be it mystical or ascetical, oral or mental, personal or communitarian, silent or vocal, private or liturgical— is not an end in itself but only a *means* that is necessary for the practice of the New Commandment, which alone ensures salvation. The other means, which is much more central in the teaching of Christ, is **self-abnegation** ("denying oneself and taking up one's cross") minus which "discipleship", i.e., "following him" in his life, death and resurrection, or experiencing the primordial salvific event, is an unachievable goal.

3. The Charismatic Experience and Liberation Theology
My first encounter with Catholic Charismatics was not a pleasant one! As a sympathizer and supporter of the ecumenically inter-religious and politically centre-left movement known as "Christian Workers Fellowship" (CWF) since 1968 —during its hay day, long before it degenerated because of a growing NGO mentality and an excessive influx of funds— I officiated as the main celebrant at their *Mass of Christ, the Worker* in a Ceramic Factory in 1974. Some members of the *Pubuduva* (as the Catholic Charismatic Movement is known to this day) started a campaign against me for allegedly preaching Marxism and conducting a scandalous liturgy! They sent a petition against me to Bp Edmund Fernando, the then interim administrator of the Colombo Diocese; he relayed the complaint to my

Provincial Fr Thomas Kuriacose. I sent a written response with a theological explanation of the Eucharist that we celebrated, demonstrating also that the signatories of the petition had not been present at that mass! The CWF later published and circulated my response here and abroad. In the meantime the factory workers argued that the real scandal was the meaningless way the Sunday masses are conducted in parishes [which some of them had stopped attending altogether] and that during the Factory Mass they regained their faith and enjoyed the service. So they sent the Bishop a counter-petition containing more signatures than those in the Charismatics' petition! My Provincial too explained matters to the Bishop giving him also the text of the mass. Since that day this Bishop has been a close friend and supporter of my work!

But a change of attitude did take place in the ranks of the Pubuduva itself, which, I had always admired and praised for having been the **world's first Charismatic movement which associated our being anointed by the Holy Spirit with our involvement in social issues** —though today there are a few groups that have departed from this sane tradition, about which I offer my critical comments below. Furthermore, the original Charismatic movement was *solely* responsible for **bringing the Word of God to the homes of the laity and for producing many biblically literate lay leaders** who employed the vernacular language in their study-cum-prayer sessions and animated the charismatic cells that mushroomed in parishes, not infrequently in conflict with the traditional parish priests and paying a price for it. It was they, and not the bishops and presbyters, who complied with the strong appeals of Vatican II's *Vebum Dei* to bring all the faithful to a personal acquaintance with the Scriptures. Thus they should be given the credit for preparing the ground for sowing the seed of an Asian Theology in our country.

After they realized that the petition written against me was the work of some misguided members of their movement, their Founding Father, the diocesan priest Fr Oscar Abeyratna together with some resident members of his Charismatic community in Ragama began to visit our (Tulana) centre) periodically for bible discussions and liturgies conducted by me. Many liturgical changes that I had introduced seeped into that of the Charismatics who, being members of a mass movement, were helpful in diffusing those liturgical elements right through the Island. Features from the lectures that I gave them at their centre or at ours were published in their journals and the ideas assimilated into their movement. Their initial rejection of popular religiosity (Marian devotions etc.) was from my perspective a serious mistake. Popular religiosity is in my view an essential ingredient of an Asian Liberation theology, as I argue later in this book. I brought this to the notice of those in charge. Things changed.

Unfortunately, however, this movement split into several factions within a couple of decades. One group met me in person to discern whether they should break away from the main group. After giving the principles of "discernment" (ignorance of which is perilous for charismatics) I pleaded that diversity, not divisiveness, is the hallmark of the Spirit. But I regret that the division did take place. At the moment I am very much at ease with groups that have faithfully committed themselves to social emancipation of the marginalized (in harmony with the *original vision* of the Pubuduva), but not so comfortable with those prayer-groups, both Roman Catholic and non-Catholic, that transport crowds into another world for a couple of hours every week *without* ever demanding a radical change in the lives of the participants specially with regard to the biblical imperative of being *for* the oppressed and being *with* the oppressed in whatever measure they could. For no Charismatic Christian

71

of any denomination can ignore the *Nazareth Manifesto in Luke 4*, which reveals that the *anointing by the Holy Spirit* confers the mission of *emancipating the oppressed* and ushering in the Year of Grace that brings reconciliation and equality through justice!

I have met a few well-meaning Charismatics (cutting across denominations) who suffer from that same hubris which is characteristic of some (not all) born-again Christians who proclaim "I am saved", but without stopping there, presume and announce that others are not! When I tried to point out the social dimension of Christian spirituality, an influential Charismatic replied, perhaps with great sincerity: "You are speaking intellectually whereas I speak from an experience of Christ!" Whether I had such an experience or not is a different matter. But the *unexamined assumption* that I who am a Religious for so many decades could not have experienced Christ came to me as a shock, echoing the words "I am not like this publican". Such well-intentioned persons possessing a zeal for the Word and doing much good, not only suffer from similar presumptions but also fear to disturb the unjust social order. They undoubtedly receive the patronage of bishops of the same frame of mind and actually need the hierarchical patronage to survive whereas other movements which are engaged in justice issues continue to utilize and enjoy the right of assembly that the Cannon Law advocates for the laity.

The other accusation broadcast is that my bible-based critique of such "other-worldly" spiritualities is purely *theoretical*! This is their verdict on Liberation Theology, which I discovered, ironically, by *doing* theology while serving the Church-neglected flock in the poorest quarters of Naples, working with youth in the suburban parish of Pozzuoli and attending to the pastoral care of sick in a hospital (Clinica Mediterranea near our Faculty*)*, and later during my doctoral

72

studies in Colombo, working in the slums of Dematagoda, and, after establishing Tulana, animating factory workers, rural youth and trade unionists, at the risk of attracting the wrath and the threats of a right-wing Member of Parliament.[44] I felt dismayed to hear from such Charismatics that this Asian liberation theology was "theoretical" or "a purely intellectual understanding of the Bible" and still claim to be possessed by the Spirit of Jesus Christ who ate and drank with marginalized. Such charismatics need to be re-evangelized!

Once when confronted by me, a member of such a group appealed to the "miracles" being witnessed to at their prayer sessions. They do not realize that such miracles occur everywhere and even in pagan shrines where God grants sincere requests made before an idol in good faith; for God sees the heart and the sincerity of those who seek relief from distress. Besides, our salvation does not depend on the miracles that we think we perform with divine help. Note that even Jesus —divine and, *therefore*, humble— attributed miracles to the faith of the persons healed rather than to himself: *your* faith has healed you. He also clearly and emphatically declared that claiming to have performed miracles is no guarantee of eternal salvation (Mt 7:22-23). The sign that he gives us is that of Jonah (Mt 12:39-40; 16:4), a hint at the death-defying way of the cross which invariably ends in the resurrection, namely the option for justice which has a crown of thorns as its reward before the crown of glory is won. This is a hard saying. This is what liberation theology is about.

The fundamental flaw in the thinking of such groups —and not of the whole movement, I concede— is, as mentioned

---

[44] See Sr Frances de Silva, RGS, *Tulana, A Jesuit Apostolate of the Sri Lanka Province*, Kelaniya 2009, pp. 24-28.

73

above, their misconception that "spirituality" is opposed to *allegedly* 'material' or 'earthly' concerns of justice and equity. This widespread view contradicts the biblical anthropology wherein the "human person", is the "Body" (*sōma*), which consists of **flesh** (*sarx*) and the mortal perishable **'soul'** (*psyche*) fortified and animated by the eternal Spirit (*to Pneuma*). Hence "spirituality" (or Spirit-animated life) is none other than both our *physical involvements* subsumed under *sarx* or "flesh" (i.e., our biological and social/secular activities) as well as *mental operations* called *psyche* (i.e., thinking, praying, planning, expressing ideas, communicating emotions etc.) both performed *under the guidance of the Holy Spirit* rather than through self-interest. Spirituality is *living out the psycho-physical* reality in a Spirit-led manner, i.e. as spiritual worship (Rom 12: 1-2). [45]

On the other hand the "prosperity gospel" allows their preachers to enjoy the best of earthly comfort,[46] which, of course, they would not condemn as 'material' but welcome as God's special blessings whereas the liberation theologian's zeal to encourage the poor and the oppressed to struggle for their legitimate share of that same blessing on earth would sound in their ears a non-spiritual enterprise. How those few who claim to be speaking under the guidance of the Holy Spirit miss this central teaching of the Bible eludes my understanding. Liberation Theology, on the other hand, offers a *holistic* understanding of liberation eschewing all dichotomies such as earthly/heavenly or material/spiritual or this-worldly/other-worldly, salvation/liberation and so on because its basis is the faith in the Biblically revealed God who is covenanted with the oppressed of *all times* and

---

[45] As explained in *Mysticism of Service*, pp. 90-97.
[46] For data see "Prosperity Gospel", *The Tablet*, 26 January 2013, p.17.

engaged with us in the project in bringing about a *new heaven and a new earth.*

4. The Holistic Perception of Liberation

The conclusion I derive from the foregoing reflections is that 'liberation' cannot be dichotomized into *spiritual* salvation and *social* deliverance. Already with the biblical studies undertaken in the late 1960s, the *unitary perception* of socio-spiritual deliverance characteristic of the Semitic mind had begun to haunt me. Some theologians (Jesuits, of course!), obviously still thinking in scholastic categories, had complained to Fr General Peter-Hans Kolvenbach that I was misleading my readers by failing to distinguish between 'salvation' (identified with soteriology) and liberation! He relayed the complaint to me in a personal hand-written letter. My response to my critics took the guise of a little book, which was eventually published as *God's Reign for God's Poor: A Return to the Jesus Formula* (Kelaniya, 1999) now available also in Spanish.[47]

But many still see double. A spoon in a half-filled glass of water *appears* bisected due to refraction; the medium that makes some theologians see double is Greek Philosophy absorbed into Christian thought! Millennial habits take long to disappear! For example, in an Indian anthology where the thinking of most contemporary theologians are each summed up *in a few pages* (!) by a person assigned to each theologian, the unnamed writer who studied my works, despite including the aforementioned book in his bibliography, ends up with the same stereotype remark, namely, that I had neglected the soteriological dimension![48] He has not taken the spoon out of

---

[47] *El Reino de Dios para los Pobres de Dios: Retorno a la Formula de Jesus*, Mensajero, Bilbao, 2006
[48] *The Contemporary Theologians: Context and Contribution*, ed. M. Illathuparambil et. al (eds), Bangalore 2006, p.389.

the water! The non-Semitic medium has misled him into a dichotomous perception of soteriology.[49]

Hence for the sake of such persons, who must be a legion, I have re-formulated the experience of liberation to be attained by us at Level One, in the following manner:

**Deliverance of the
rich from** [the lure of] **their riches,
the poor from** [the burden of] **their poverty
and both *classes* from greed.**

This formula appropriates and develops the fundamental teaching of the Bible summed up in the Book of Proverbs in the form of a prayer:

> Two things I ask you, O Lord and do not refuse me before I die:- Keep falsehood and lies far from me; **give me neither poverty nor riches, but give me only my daily bread.** Otherwise I may have too much and disown you and say, "Who is the Lord?" Or I may become poor and steal and so dishonor the name of my God. (Prov. 30: 7-9)

The message given here is that both poverty and riches are undesirable in God's sight. Hence in the definition of liberation given above, **social** emancipation (i.e., elimination of *classes*) and **personal** liberation (elimination of *greed*) are **indivisibly absorbed into each other** because of the following two reasons:-

(a) the elimination of *classes* ("structural" revolution) is not complete unless and until the "class mentality"

---

[49] I have dealt with this issue in greater detail in my article, "Revisiting Faith and Justice Mission: One More Appeal for a Paradigm Shift", *The Third Millennium,* Jan-March 2012, pp. 5-20; reprinted as chapter II in my *Our Unhidden Agenda:* pp. 20-35.

of both the rich and the poor is also eradicated
("cultural" revolution); for God who took a relatively
short time to free the Israelites from Egyptian
slavery, took forty years to liberate them from their
slave-mentality;

(b) the elimination of <u>greed</u> in individuals alone is not
sufficient to bring a greedless society because greed
is organized into a global movement governed by
the Market which is scripturally identifiable as
"Mammon" (Mt 6:24;Lk 16:9) or the "Ruler of this
World" (Jn 16:11) or the "Adversary" (Mt 4:1,5,8)
or the [Attractive] "Beast" (Rev. 14:11 and *passim*).
Hence a *communitarian struggle* against the
principalities and the powers of this ubiquitous Idol
is presupposed in our notion of liberation. This
struggle is not one of violence even in the face of
violence; but a non-violent *resistance* said of the
Suffering Servant in Isaiah (50: 5-9) as well as
persistence in defying persecution and even death
through an uncompromised faith. (see section 8
below)

Thus in sharing Christ's struggle to usher in and spread
God's Reign, wherein both *greed* and *need* are to disappear,
we must follow "Deutero-Paul" (Col. 3:5; Eph 5:5) in
identifying "greed" (*pleonexia*) as "creature-worship"
(*eidololatria*) or an anti-God option, so that both the theistic
and non-theistic religionists could concur in identifying the
sin from which liberation is sought: "idolatry" or "addiction
to creatures" in theistic religions and "greed" (or slavish
dependence on transitory things) in non-theistic religions.
According to Ex. 20:3 (I am the Lord your God who freed
you from the house of bondage in Egypt and [*therefore*],
have no other gods before me) the worship of the one
liberator-God coincides with our non-greed, i.e., our refusal

77

to be addicted to or to be enslaved by all human-made and
God-made creatures. This does not refer solely to a personal
and interior liberation of each and every person. There is also
the social and structural dimension of liberation, which is
featured in our dogged insistence on the liberation of *both the
rich and the poor* and which points to the primary role that
the **class factor** plays in liberation theology. This is what we
are about to discuss now:-

5. Primacy of *Class factor* over both *Gender* and *Race* in Liberation Theology

We believe firmly that in Christ (Gal 3:28) —and therefore,
in Christianity, too— any discrimination in terms of *gender*
(male/female), *race* (Jew/Gentile) and *class* (Slave/Free) is
intolerable as it should also be in any society on earth. Note,
however, that among these three areas of prejudice, the **class
bias** is the **foundational** one. It is at the root of the other two
forms of discrimination. The reason is obvious. Gender is a
biological datum and Race is an *ethnological* datum. They
are both gifts of Nature. **God is the author of gender
difference and ethnic diversity**. But **class stratification** into
haves and have-nots **is the monstrous creation of
Mammon,** the Undistributed Wealth, God's opposite
number. It is the fruit of sin. By making this assertion I am
laying down what I consider to be a *basic presupposition in
any theology of liberation.*

Some Asian feminists and certain Tamils have
misapprehended my exploration into Asian Liberation
theology because they had seriously neglected the role of the
class factor (i.e., the **economic structures**) in *gender* and
race conflicts.

Some Asian **feminists** who criticized me in the 1980s for
allegedly neglecting women's issues in "my" theology, were

unaware that I was handling this subject in my lectures at the EAPI in Manila to multinational Asian audiences at least a decade before those same Asian feminists even became conscious of feminism! Secondly I was not parroting Western feminist perspectives but presented an Asian version of it. I confess, however, that it was my feminist students in the Union Theological Seminary, New York that educated me in the use of inclusive language.

I have vindicated my position on **class-infected feminism** in the book *Fire and Water*, where I have presented a summary of those Manila lectures.[50] In fact one of the few *Asian* feminists who have recognized the class factor in their gender-discourse is, ironically, an edifyingly Indianized *German* lady, Prof. Dr Gabriele Dietrich who is heavily involved in the mass struggles of the most exploited among her Indian sisters!! On the other hand I have heard of bourgeois Asian feminists who have maid-servants to slave for them in a feudal set-up, both in households and in convents! No wonder they had been so blinded by the gender issues as to be impervious to the class factor in the exploitation of women. In my theological explorations I paid special attention to the class stratification, the neglect of which has led some Asian feminists into a blind alley.

This same phenomenon is observed in those engaged in the struggle for **inter-racial justice** with no attention paid to the *class* issue. The cowardly "diaspora Sinhalese" who dream of establishing a New Sinhala Rājya in Sri Lanka from a comfortable distance are matched by a few Lankan Tamil presbyters who have migrated to Europe in search of greener pastures for themselves after deserting their suffering co-nationals during the height of the ethnic crisis but are now

---

[50] *Fire and Water, Basic Issues in Asian Buddhism and Christianity*, Orbis Books, Marknoll, 1996, Chapters 1-6. **(Hence forward *Fire and Water*)**

seeking the liberation of Sri Lankan Tamils through a remote-control mechanism. It is these latter whohave accused me of not including the "ethnic issue" in my Liberation theology! For they, too, belong to a particular *class* and their response to the racism of Sinhala extremists is equally race-centered. There was just one Tamil group, the one led by Umar Maheshwaram, who, though committed to violence, —or more precisely, to counter violence— was profoundly aware of the class basis of the ethnic conflict; but that particular faction of the Tamil liberation movement was ruthlessly persecuted by the LTTE, whose struggle for justice was race-based to the neglect of the class factor. On the other hand the whole world knows and admires those heroic Tamil Shepherds (whose names I withhold for their own safety) who have risked and continue to risk their lives even today in accompanying their flock 'through death's dark valley'.

I have hurled the same challenge to the Sinhala 'liberationists" of the JVP *Janatha Vimukthi Peramuna* or People's Liberation Front, since the late 1980s. Unfortunately many Sinhalese, even Christians among them, were guilty of chauvinism. Though there is a conversion noticed in recent times, the JVPiers were also racists who did not have "class comrades" on the Tamil side *at that time*. The biblical poor are basically the *slave-class,* whose labour is exploited by the *leisure class.* The **fisher-folk, small land-holding farmers, estate labourers, factory workers and miners who *cut across the racial and gender divide* were ignored *as a class* by those who fought for equality with a narrow focus on ethnicity.**

For Liberation Theology is basically inspired by the biblical notion of the poor as an enslaved *class,* who gradually became a People (*'am*), i.e., more than a mere Nation ($g\hat{o}y$). Against the mistaken theory that "the Sinhala and the Tamil *people*" are actually "enemy *nations*", we have consistently proposed the alternative thesis that victims of injustice are the exploited *class* of both Sinhalese and the Tamils forming a majority whereas victimizers are an elite *class* of individuals racially comprising both Sinhalese and Tamils. This is the approach we advocate even today against the racist politics of extremists on either side. In fact, who are the culprits persecuting the Tamil masses in the North of Sri Lanka today (2009-2012)? Are they not a social class consisting of Sinhala Administrators and Tamil Collaborators?

By no means do I deny the importance of gender and race issues. What I hold is that class-discrimination, which the Scriptures censure as unbecoming of believers in Our Lord Jesus Christ (Jas 2:1-5), remains the framework within which the gender and race discriminations should be perceived and *consequently* contested and eventually eliminated. Minus that, no theology is liberational.

Since the late 1970s and early 1980s, I have been conducting at our Tulana Centre and elsewhere a non-stop series of seminars for Sinhala rural youth and workers as well as trade unionists on the Buddhist-Christian approach to socio-political issues with *special emphasis on the ethnic issue*. Our method, essentially an inter-religious one, was a combination of historical study and social analysis grounded in the Sacred Scriptures of religions, specially the Tripitaka and the Bible. Groups and groups of Sinhalese (both Buddhists and Christians) have been conscientized about the Tamil grievances based on facts and data culled from the country's history. My Tamil critics in the North, now in Europe, joined by a few Tamils in Tamilnadu (who too have adopted a racial rather than a class approach to this question) were not only ignorant of our work of reconciliation, but also   failed to supplement our efforts with a corresponding study of the history of Sinhala fears of the Tamils, specially the fears resulting from the disastrous Chola (Tamil) invasion which

81

devastated 13 centuries of Sinhala Buddhist Culture by laying waste the Anuradahapura Kingdom and about the bloody pogrom unleashed by hooligans led by Magha of Indian origin, which burnt down Buddhist monasteries and their libraries, dispersing the Sinhala Buddhists (monks and the laity) to other parts of the country and even outside the country as refugees. The Pali literature of the period refers to this event as the great conflagration. The Sinhala-Buddhists have never recovered from this shock. There is a dangerous memory operating in them about the past Tamil aggressions and a fear of facing similar ones in the future. In a paper I read at the CCA conference on "Peoples' Movements" held in Singapore in 1982 (one year before the anti-Tamil pogrom of Black July), I argued that the Chola invasion was undertaken for mere political and economical motives rather than on ethno-religious grounds, and warned that even then a racio-religious persecution can be (and has been) read into it because the aggressors were Tamil-Hindus from India and the victims were Sinhala-Buddhists of Lanka.[51]

The Tamils have to be sensitive enough to respond constructively to these fears. Educating the Tamils to understand the aforementioned section of the Island's history as well as the "minority complex" of the Sinhalese majority in the face of 50 million Tamils in the region had never been taken up seriously by many of the Tamil Clergy —barring a few exceptions, of course. Hence some of us who worked on this important mission of educating the Sinhalese to acquire a sane approach towards the Tamils had, if at all, only a handful of collaborators on the other side, but we had many armchair critics who did not care or dare to do the same foundational work among the Tamils that we were doing among the Sinhalese. None of these critics has ever lived

---

[51] "Buddhist Political Visioning in Sri Lanka" in: Preman Niles, ed., *Towards the Sovereignty of the People*, CCA, Singapore, 1983, pp.132-145.

with us to know what we have been doing!! The reason? They sought a *racial* liberation without questioning the *class* conflict that infected the Tamil society —a failure which was partly responsible for the military defeat of the Tigers; for a *class* of Tamils who felt discriminated by the dominant class in the LTTE itself switched allegiance to the Sinhala Government's side!

Both parties in conflict, specially those professing the Christian faith on either side, failed to realize the biblical significance of *the land,* which has been the bone of contention. The biblical notion of liberation placed a high value on the *means of production* which, at that time, as in today's ethnic conflict, was/is *the land.* Biblical laws of justice in Leviticus 25 were geared to eliminate a *class structure* that invariably springs from the "economics" of the private ownership of the land (i.e. the means of production). The commandments of God were legal expressions ($mišpāṭ$) of divine justice ($s^edāqāh$) and therefore, according to Deuteronomy 15:4-6, God promises that if these commandments were scrupulously observed, there would be no class of poor (and by implication, no class of rich) in Israel — and, I would say, in any society. The class issue is fundamental to the project of liberation. Regrettably, both the Tamils and the Sinhalese were fighting a *racial* war; and both parties have lost it. The conflict has spread to the diaspora, where well-to-do expatriates of both the ethnic groups (exceptions granted) are obsessed mostly by racial concerns.

6. From "Inculturation-Liberation paradigm" to "Poverty-Religiosity paradigm"

The inculturation-liberation debate was and is another area where *a lack of class analysis* has resulted in an impasse. Inculturation is a natural process that any religion undergoes when it tries to survive in a culture other than the one in which it had originated. A natural process cannot be induced

83

artificially. It would be tantamount to a conscious effort at being spontaneous. Rather, the question that needs to be asked is *in which class* of the host-nation has the adherents of the guest-religion incarnated itself. If there is an oppressive hierarchy in a religion then a class difference has already set in. In most Asian countries, the Christian clerics, even if recruited initially from the poorer stratum of society, have ended up being *culturally absorbed into the elite class*. Thus the Asian churches are characterized by **a class structure** —a fruit of an inculturation. This is most evident in Asian countries that have been previously colonized by Western nations that claimed to be Christian. It is once again the failure to take into account the class conflict in Asian societies that prevented many Asian theologians from seeing the danger of every form of inculturation that neglects to incarnate the **liberative core of one's own religion** in the host-culture in harmony with the **libertative core of religions indigenous to the host culture**.

This is why I have been consistently appealing to my colleagues that our focus in Asia should be on both the **enslaving and the liberating facets of *religions*** that permeates our cultures **rather than on those cultures** as such.

The early history of Western Christianity has taught us enough lessons about this phenomenon. When the message of the Gospels, which the poor class in Israel received from Jesus and his apostles, spread through the Roman Empire, it was the *Greek-speaking racially hybrid class of an urbanized elite* that first received the seed of the Gospel. The kind of Christianity that grew up from this seed was, therefore, *culturally stamped* by the social mores and the Hellenistic mind-set of that **elite class** —specially with regard to the subordination of slaves to masters and women to men, as we notice already in the pastoral letters. The first Christian communities were household churches and were beholden to that same class which provided large homes for their liturgies. St Paul makes a clear condemnatory reference to the class distinction in the house-church in Corinth (I Cor 11:17-22). But the upper class seemed to have monopolized the church leadership in the subsequent decades and centuries.

The first Greek Councils climaxing in Chalcedon's doctrine of incarnation reveals a form of *inculturation* in the thought patterns and social *mores* of Greco-Roman elite class of the Empire. They did not seem to have acknowledged the centrality of the *liberation brought by the crucified Christ*! It was a Christology minus soteriology! That was the severe verdict of Cardinal Alois Grilmeyer, the Chalcedon specialist (see Chapter VII). It is this species of **non-liberationally inculturated** theology **stuffed** **with** **philosophical speculation** that is being employed even today by the Central Bureau of the Western Patriarchate as the criterion of orthodoxy to pass its judgment on liberation theologians who strive to preach the Crucified and Risen Christ! Many seminaries in Asia continue to teach the aforementioned theology which has already failed in the West at least since the enlightenment if not earlier. The policy we see in the Centre of Catholicism, as amply illustrated in the CDF's *Dominus Jesus*, is not one of laying the axe to the root of the tree that has ceased to bear fruit, but to replace Asia's fruit-bearing trees with that dead stump.[52]

Some Asian theologians, instead of learning a lesson from this narrow and inane policy of the Western Patriarchate, had tried to duplicate this same species of *non-liberational inculturation* in their countries. The efforts at indigenization of Christian worship in South Asia has been dubbed by the

---

[52] For an Asian evaluation of *Dominus Jesus*, see *Give Vatican II a Chance : Yes to Incessant Renewal, No to Reform of the Reforms*, Kelaniya, 2010 Chapter V. (**Hence forward *Give Vatican II a Chance*)**

85

oppressed classes as 'Brahmanization'; the effort to theologize in terms of Vedantic thought resulted in an Indic scholasticism that outdid its Western precedent based on Greek philosophy. The *cosmic religiosity* of the "ordinary masses" or the *ochlos* of the Gospel (which I discuss in detail in the next Chapter), have not been allowed to offer their *this-worldly liberative character* to the ethereal theologies that many Asians were manufacturing despite the fact that the cosmic genre of Asian religiosity resonated to a great extent with the Semitic idiom of *biblical* soteriology.

It is for this reason that I avoided the futile debate between Inculturationism and Liberationism and proposed to the ATC (ASIAN THEOLOGICAL CONSULTATION) of the EATWOT (ECUMENICAL ASSOCIATION OF THIRD WORLD THEOLOGIANS) in 1979 *another theological language* based on the two poles of Asian Cultures: *religiosity and poverty,* each taken in its "enslaving" as well as "liberating" versions. I did not arrive at this scheme through a rational process of theorizing but *after an experience* of confronting the two realities in a Buddhist context as I had narrated in many places,[53] and "reading" *Jesus Christ,* God's Word, in the context of that experience as a revelation of his **two baptisms** (one at the Jordan under an Asian Guru in the company of very simple and humble people and the other at Calvary as a victim of violence amidst publicly acknowledged sinners),[54] this being the primary sense in which "baptism" is used in the Gospels. My appeal was that the Church in Asia too undergo this double baptism.[55] (see chart on p.87)

---

[53] See, e.g., *Prophetic Humour,* Chapter II.
[54] *ATL,* Chapter 4.
[55] *Prophetic Humour,* pp. 8-21.

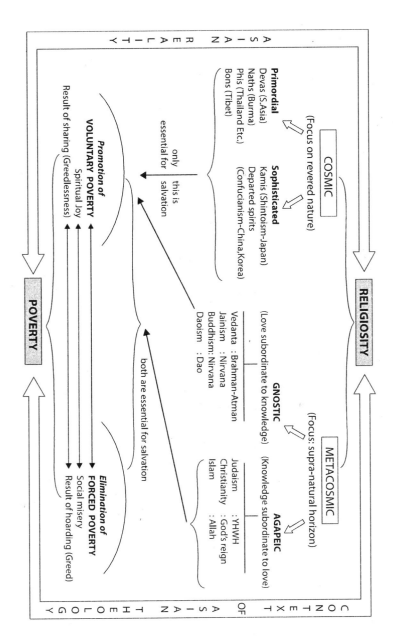

87

My controversy with my close Jesuit friend Paul Caspersz (in *Voices of the Third World,* 1980) was intended to correct his attempt to force *Asian poverty* into the 'liberation' slot and *Asian religiosity* into the 'inculturation' slot; for I was pleading with my colleagues to *replace* the "inculturation-liberation" paradigm with the "poverty-religiosity" paradigm. Two years of debate was brought to a close at the EATWOT's Tri-Continental Meeting held in Delhi in 1981, when a broad consensus was reached on my ATC proposal of 1979 —though many Western scholars, ignorant of the history of this development and of my ardent appeal to EATWOT to reject that scheme, have wasted volumes of paper interpreting my alleged use of that obsolete scheme in 'my' theology! [56]

My thesis, let me emphasize, was/is pivoting around these two mutually inclusive principles:-

1. A **RELIGIOSITY** that encourages *social poverty* directly (by associating with the ideology of the upper class) or indirectly (by not being involved in its elimination) is **enslaving;**

2. But a **RELIGIOSITY** that encourages *evangelical poverty* (which liberates one from Greed, ...greed which leads to unshared riches and class-divisions,) and thus promotes the elimination of social poverty as an intrinsically soteriological imperative, is **liberating.**

---

[56] E.g., cf. Mario Bellemare's post-graduate Dissertation, *Prophetic Asceticism in the Wilderness, Dilemmas of the Liberation-Inculturation Paradigm of Aloysius Pieris,* Mc Gill University, Montreal, Quebec, Canada. 1998

88

Conversely,

1. **Evangelical POVERTY** (non-idolatrous or greedless living) which is a "sign" of God's Reign (or salvation) is a **liberative** praxis that has close parallels in every Asian Religion, Christian and non-Christian, though couched in different cultural idioms;

2. But **Social POVERTY** is a "counter-sign" of God's Reign (or salvation) because it is **enslaving.** The Asian religions including Christianity that refuse to combat this structural evil (which is born of institutional greed or globalized mammonolatry) become themselves enslaving.

Hence, liberation theology is derived from the **baptismal praxis** of *becoming evangelically poor* and simultaneously of *joining the socially poor in their struggle for freedom.* The implication is that "option *to be* poor" and "option *for* the poor" are an inseparable commitment of *all* Christians. This is a position much misinterpreted by *liberal* theologians and needs to be re-stated with precision as I am about to do in the very next section.

7. Theological Implications of the Two-fold Praxis
It follows from the above that the Asian theology we advocate is one that combines *in its praxis* the liberative dimension of both poverty and religiosity and a relentless struggle to reduce their enslaving aspects. Here, the central teaching of all Asian religions (*option to be poor* or evangelical poverty) is incorporated into an Asian theology while not compromising the **unique mission specific to Biblical Christianity**, namely, a praxis based on the belief that the elimination of social poverty (*option for the poor* or commitment to erase or at least reduce "class differentiation"

in society) is a **constitutive dimension of salvation** —on a par with evangelical poverty, which is not exclusive to Christianity. If we neglect this unique mission of joining the oppressed in their struggle, in any measure possible, we lose our identity as Christians (as argued out in Chapter VIII).

On the other hand, engagement in the liberation of the poor *without* a concomitant practice of evangelical poverty is the accepted policy of many aid agencies and charitable organizations wherein a *disproportionate* amount of financial resources meant for the poor are wasted on maintaining the aid-agency itself (desk-work, salaries for the staff, etc.) and the organizers of such projects are criticized, quite justifiably, for living on the poor rather than serving them. In some ways this is a replica of the World Bank model of aiding poor countries. This model, unfortunately, is visibly operative in many Church run aid agencies. The socially poor, whom such agencies claim to serve, do not see in those who work in these agencies men and women who are evangelically poor.

I have personally experienced the attitude of Asia's socially poor to Asia's evangelically poor in 1971 during my Tertianship [a third year of novitiate made at the end of a Jesuit's long formation]. I used the time of the "experiment" (an Ignatian exercise of *experiencing* various challenges of life) to travel on foot and mule, by bus and train from Bombay in the West coast of India across the Gangetic valley to Nalanda in the East, and back to Ahamadabad in the West; I made this tediously long journey clad *a la* "Sanyasi" (a world-renouncer) sleeping in railway stations, public buildings and road sides, but was never allowed to starve thanks to the generosity of the Indian poor who were practising a cosmic spirituality.[57]

---

[57] See *Prophetic Humour*, Chapter I.

Chart II: Bidimensionality of Liberation

EXAMPLES ↓	OPTION TO BE POOR Promotion of Voluntary Poverty (personal practice of beatitudes)	OPTION FOR THE POOR Elimination of Forced Poverty (collective struggle for justice)
biblically inadequate some Christian ashrams; some monastic and religious Houses	**YES** They concentrate on personal holiness by practicing and witnessing to the beatitudinal spirituality of Jesus. This spirituality is not unique to Christianity; it is the common spirituality that Christians share with all other religionists .	**NO** They fail to realize that this is a constitutive as well as distinctive dimension of biblical Christianity; a mark of the true church as are "holiness', "unity" etc.. Christians must co-opt adherents of Gnostic religions to join them in this mission, which is not obligatory for them but does not contradict their teachings.
biblically questionable most NGOs, many Christian Charities and other aid agencies	**NO** A good part of the money meant for the poor is spent on maintaining the aid agencies and a highly paid staff.	**YES** *but* They serve the poor as benefactors rather than as partners in a common struggle. Identification with the oppressed is wanting.
biblically condemned "Rich Fool" & "Dives" in Luke; plutocrats who rule the world today	**NO** Hoarding or gathering which Jesus repudiates in the Sermon on the Mount	**NO** Greedy who refuse to share even their excess possessions with the Needy who starve at their door step.
biblically prescribed MOSES/ JESUS	**YES** Moses renounced wealth, prestige and power as a necessary prelude to his mission to liberate the slaves (OT)	**YES** By opting for the oppressed, Moses exercised his faith and opted for Christ (Hebr. 11:24) for faith in God and justice to the poor go together in biblical Christianity.
Cistercian Monks of Algeria Many "Basic Christian Communities" in the Third World	Jesus, who renounced his family and job, had no place of his own to be born in, to lay his head on or to be buried in; he practiced the beatitudes which he preached. (NT)	In word and deed, Jesus defended the dignity of the religiously condemned, integrated the socially ostracized, and restored health and life to those deprived of them; he also repudiated structural sin.

91

The symbol of the renouncer is a highly visible reminder of the core message of all Asian religions. And quite a few Christian monks, both Western and Asian, have bravely witnessed to it in their life-style here in Asia. Note on the other hand that through such life-testimonies of Christian ascetics, male and female, who have *opted to be (evangelically) poor,* the church witnesses only to one half of its mission, namely, solidarity with the **common spirituality of all religions.** This needs to be complemented by an *option for the (socially) poor,* minus which the **distinctive spirituality of biblical Christianity** is neither proclaimed nor practiced. Whereas *some* Christian aid agencies do not witness to evangelical poverty while being engaged in the service of those condemned to socially poverty, *some* Ashramic and monastic centres do the converse: practice evangelical poverty without committing themselves to socially poor.

The need for both options was brought very clearly in the Third International Monastic Congress (Kandy, Sri Lanka, 1980) and was the essence of their final statement.[58] The Cistercian Monks of Algiers have now left a precedent that cannot be ignored because they sealed the two-fold option with their blood. I return to the consequences of this option in Chapters VII and VIII.

This explains why our aforementioned definition of liberation encompasses a reduction (if not an elimination) of class differences through the deliverance of the rich from their riches as well as the deliverance of the poor from their poverty. The ideal implied, here, is "equity" or "fair balance" as explained below in the words of St Paul. Its aim is not only to eliminate *social poverty* which is indicative of a

---

[58] "Message to the Asian Communities: The Final Statement of the Kandy Conference, *Dialogue NS,* Vol. VII, No. 3 (Sep-Dec. 1980), pp. 119-121; 137.

class structure, but also to deliver both the rich and the poor from greed through practice and promotion of *evangelical poverty*. A society where there is none having *too much* and none having *too little* is a sign of God's Reign, for such a society cannot emerge without a diminishment, if not a total elimination, of acquisitiveness and greed through a social enactment of the evangelical principle of **equity** or **fair balance** (*isotēs* in Greek)

St Paul conveys this message of *isotēs* (**equity** or **fair balance**) cogently to the rich Corinthians when he appealed to them to reduce the difference between their plenty and the Jerusalem community's penury. Here is how he puts it in 2 Cor 8:13-15:-

> I do not mean that there should be relief for others and pressure on you, but it is a question of *equity* [a **fair balance**] between your present abundance and their need so that their abundance may be for your need, in order that there may be *equity* [a **fair balance**]. As it is written "The one who had much did not have *too much*, and the one who had little did not have *too little*".

8. Debt Cancellation (or Forgiveness) and Reconciliation in an *Asian* Theology

The language barrier between biblical soteriology and other religions in Asia is nowhere so difficult to break through as in the use of the three biblical expressions mentioned above. But we have a precedent to follow, as demonstrated in No. 4 above; there we have already broken down another wall of incomprehension when Deutero-Paul's equation of **idolatry** with **greed** (Col 3:5;Eph 5:5) led us to recognize the Buddhists' *anti-idolatrous spirituality of "non-greed"* as the homologue (not equivalent) of biblical Christianity's *refusal* to *worship any 'god' other than YHWH* (Ex.20:3) —YHWH Whom we Christians firmly believe to be a God

93

covenanted with the oppressed,[59] so that the commitment to the **practice of evangelical poverty** ("greedlessness" for Buddhists and "worship of the One True God" for Christians) needs *necessarily* to be accompanied by the commitment to the **elimination of social poverty** preferably with Buddhist participation.[60] This clarification has enabled Buddhists and Christians to share the concern for personal and social liberation as a common enterprise. This methodology is to be employed, *mutatis mutandis,* in our collaboration also with other non-Christians.

This same process of dialogue would help Buddhists (and other non-Christian collaborators) to understand within *their* own specific idiom why we Christians consider the **Jubilee law of Debt-cancellation as well as its synonyms** (*forgiveness* and *reconciliation*) as pointing to the kind of liberation that both we and they seek. Here below are some clarifications we arrived at in dialogue with Buddhist activists over many years.

Some Theravada Buddhists (whose stance does not differ from that of the adherents of non-theistic religions such as Vedantic Hinduism and Jainism) have declared that they are not comfortable with the words "forgiveness" and "reconciliation",[61] and *a fortiori,* with the "Jubilee Law of Debt-Cancellation". Such concepts, at first sight, seem to contradict their belief in *karmic* retribution. If I forgive someone, it is I who practice compassion and gain some footage in the long journey through *saṃsāra* (cycle of rebirth) but the offender, despite being forgiven by me, is not thereby liberated from his or her sin which has to be expiated

---

[59] See *Unhidden Agenda,* pp.52-54
[60] As demonstrated at length by means of a cross-scripture study in *Prophetic Humour,* pp. 90-100.
[61] See "Forgiveness, A Daring Human Achievement", (Editorial), *Dialogue NS,* xxix (2002), p. i.

in this or in a future birth.[62] **Hence the categorical rejection of "divine forgiveness" and a "forgiving God" is to be respected as a non-negotiable factor in such non-theistic religions.**

On the other hand the search for **"forgiveness" and "reconciliation"** between God and humans as well as among humans is of the **very essence of *Christian* soteriology**. In fact, the Holy Spirit, the supreme gift of the Crucified-Risen Christ to us, is a *divine person identified with the forgiveness of our sins* (as we confess in our Credo every Sunday); but this reference is not merely to God's forgiveness of *my* sins, but also the *salvific power* by which *we forgive those who sin against us*. The Spirit turns our words of forgiveness into divine speech-commands so that those whom we forgive here on earth are forgiven in heaven, as promised by the Risen Saviour. We can liberate others from the sins they commit against us. This belief has **no equivalent** in the three religions mentioned above and, therefore, we have to look for a **homologue** that can break the language barrier. An *Asian liberation theology* has to assimilate *other Asian perceptions of liberation* advocated by other Asian soteriologies. How greedlessness —*their* term for liberation— is intended in such words as "reconciliation", "forgiveness" and "debt-cancellation" still remains a hurdle to clear in our dialogue with non-Christians in Asia. This has been an area of endless conversation that challenges the Asian theologian.[63] Let me repeat that what follows is a summary of what I have learnt during the many sessions I had conducted over many decades to bring about inter-ethnic *reconciliation* in the context of inter-religious and ecumenical conversations.

---

[62] It is true that in popular Buddhism or cosmic Buddhism, even in Sri Lanka, there are people who recite a prayer seeking pardon from the Buddha for their sins; but this practice is not considered orthodox.

[63] See the entire issue of *Dialogue NS,* xxxv-xxxvi (2008-2009) where this question is discussed in terms of justice and human rights.

The first lesson I learnt was that Christians themselves are confused by very hazy notions surrounding the typically biblical term **"debt-cancellation"** which is synonymous with reconciliation and forgiveness (or *peace through justice*). It is none other than the Nazareth Manifesto of Jesus in Luke 4. The OT (Leviticus and Deuteronomy) presents *debt cancellation* as a means of maintaining social equality (or "fair balance" to use Paul's term cited above) or preventing a class stratification; here, our Christian understanding of Buddhist greedlessness, as explained above, has helped us to work on a common understanding of social justice implied in debt-cancellation. In Buddhism sharing (*saṃvibhāgo*) is the antidote to hoarding (*bahubhāṇḍa-vāda*). Debt-cancellation is a concrete mechanism which ensures equity or fair balance through sharing (leading to fair distribution of goods and services). Thus the language barrier has been broken at least among activists of both religions in this matter.

But this OT teaching on debt-cancellation has been transformed by an *added significance which Jesus had introduced* into it through his life, ministry and teaching. As a Jesus-follower, therefore, my first step is to confess in word and deed that "debt-cancellation" *also* implies that *I hold no one to be indebted to me,* and that the *indebtedness* which I am called to renounce is twofold:

   (a) the **gratitude I demand** for a *favour* I have done to my friend;
   (b) the **forgiveness I withhold** for a *wrong* I have suffered from my enemy.

Cancelling these two debts implies that we renounce any *right* to make these two demands from our friends and foes respectively. This was the sum and substance of Jesus' teaching proclaimed in word and deed on the Cross when he breathed upon us the Holy Spirit, i.e. God's redeeming Love :- [Be ready to] *die for your friends* and *forgive your enemies* [as I have done on Calvary]. This is the ideal that the gospels name *agape*, which is a Divine Person revealed as the Holy Spirit, whom we proclaim in the Credo every Sunday as the source and the author of "the holy catholic church, the communion of saints, **forgiveness** of sins, the resurrection of the body and the life everlasting". *Our final liberation is the Holy Spirit in action with us and within us.*

This further means that *reconciliation* cannot be the initiative of the offender, who cannot *buy* forgiveness with sacrifices, fasts, prayers and other works of the law (*contra* 2 Macabees, 1:5; 5:20, 7:33; 9:20)[64] but is entirely the initiative of the *offended party* —perhaps among humans, too (Mt 5:23-24)? What is intended in the only five NT *loci* where the word "reconciliation" occurs,[65] seems to be that it is God, *the Offended One,* who initiates the process of reconciliation with the repentant *human offender.* It is not a case of sinner's repentance procuring divine forgiveness; rather God's forgiving love, i.e. Her *fore-given* love takes effect when the sinner repents (Rom 2:4). We, too, are summoned by Jesus to imitate his Father's "perfection" (Mt 5:48) which is Her "mercifulness" (Lk 6:36) in offering unconditional forgiveness to those that offend us. This is the message of love that Jesus has asked us to "teach all nations"; just as founders of other religion, too, have done ... perhaps in a different idiom. Though at *the experiential level,* love is the only universally understood language, yet walls of incomprehension mushroom partly because the concept of love often suffers from the *interpretations* to which the Collective Memory is subjected to, i.e., from our theologies.

---

[64] See "What on Earth is God Doing with Us? A Search for Authentic Christian Theism", *Gleanings,* Jan-June, 2008, pp. 9 ff.
[65] *Katallagenai* in Rom 5:10-11; 11:15; 2 Cor 5: 18-20; *apokatalasso* in Col 1:20-22; Eph 2:16.

Hence an inter-religious conversation which allows *experience* (first level) to interpret the Collective Memory (second level) is an indispensable means of minimizing the language barrier. The following is a process that some of us have gone through in the early stages of inter-faith collaboration. It illustrates the fruit of a Christian-Buddhist conversation, and is applicable also in relation to other *non-theistic religions* mentioned above.

In my search for a Buddhist homologue for Christian *agape* (self-transcendent or other-centred love, which is redemptive) I found a clue in the way that *philia* (love between friends) was handled by biblical authors. "Friendship" (*philia* or Thomism's *amor amicitiae*) was the purest love that many non-Christian writers of antiquity could think of; but to the early Christians it seemed insufficiently expressive of Christian *Agape / Caritas*. But later, we see a change in the fourth gospel: the Johanine Jesus *seems* to have employed the concept of *philia* to express *agape* ("greater than which" there is no other love) by defining it as *dying for one's friend* (Jn 15:13). A Christian vocation is not merely to love the neighbor as oneself, but to love the other more than one's own life, i.e. to love as Jesus loved us (Jn13:34) by treating us as his friends at a cost to his own self. Furthermore Jesus in questioning Peter thrice about his love for his Master (Jn 21:15-17,) uses *agapan* in the first two questions and *philein* in the last one, but Peter in his response uses *philein* for all the three occurrences! Here too what is suggested by John *seems to me* to be consistent with the previous instance of transforming *philia* by redefining it in terms of *agape.* *Philein* is elevated to mean the love with which Jesus loved us as his "friends". So I presume.

I also see a similar procedure in the Buddhist Scriptures. *Mettā* ("friendly love", derived from *mitta* meaning 'friend') corresponds to *philia* of the Greeks, *amicitia* of the Latins

98

and *amor amicitiae* of Thomism. *Mettā* is regarded as *non-salvific*, i.e., not capable of mediating Nirvana. For the Final and Supreme Liberation (*Nirvana*) is attainable only through wisdom (*paññā*), supra-mundane knowledge, whereas *mettā*, as Lamotte had observed, "is not directly oriented towards detachment",[66] for detachment is a *sine qua non* for attaining freedom from greed. It is a species of friendship in which a certain amount of attachment or bonding is presupposed, whereas Nirvana is freedom from all bonds (*yogakkhema*). But in the famous discourse, Sigālovāda Sutta, the Buddha speaks of a *Kalyāna Mitta*, "the True Friend" whose friendly love is such that his very life is already sacrificed for the other" (*jīvitamp'assa pariccattaṃ hoti*). Such species of self-sacrificing love, which is more than *mettā* because it involves detachment from one's life itself, seems to be a homologous approximation to agapeic love advocated by Jesus —emphasize *homologous* (not identical), and *approximation* (not equivalence).

This observation is reinforced by the apophatic language that the Pali Canon employs in the stock phrase which "defines" so to say, the final liberation: namely, "non-possessiveness (*alobha*), non-hate (*ạdosa*) and (*amoha*) non-delusion". Note that *amoha* (negation of ignorance or delusion) is synonymous with salvific knowledge or wisdom (*paññā*) according to Buddhist scriptures; yet in Nirvana, this saving wisdom (*paññā* or *amoha*) is accompanied by the total **absence of "possessiveness" (*lobha*)** as well as the **absence of "hatred" (*dosa*) even towards enemies.** *Lobha*, often substituted by *rāga* (lust) is the equivalent of *eros* of the Greeks and *amor concupiscentiae* of Thomas. Hence the Nirvanic experience as explained by the Buddha comes across to the Christians as **Wisdom** accompanied by **Selfless**

---

[66] Etienne Lamotte, quoted in : B. de Give *A Trappist Meeting a Monk in Tibet*, Greenwing, Herefordshire, 2010, p. 279.

Love (*alobha, arāga*) and by '**Forgiving Love** (*adosa*). Our dialogue with activists ("engaged Buddhists") has made us realize that, here, too the language barrier could be broken. This may sound no more than mental jugglery to the reader; but to those of us who have dialogued on this issue with activist Buddhists in the course of a common engagement in the liberational project, this has been a significant breakthrough in the search for a Buddhist homologue of debt-cancellation, forgiveness and reconciliation.

Let me reiterate that this is the fruit of many conversations I/we have had with several Buddhist-Christian groups of activists in the late seventies and early eighties. Doctrinal reciprocity and complementariness, if not also consensus, has to be a byproduct of Buddhist-Christian *involvement* in inter-human reconciliation and forgiveness. Thus it is through engagement in works of justice that the Christian theologian can discover a common soteriological platform with our Asian neighbours, who profess other religions.[67] This remains the only effective methodology in Asia.

9. Liberative Non-Violence that Hurts the Oppressor

Liberal theologians and the Western Patriarch's guardians of orthodoxy seem to "see red" and "smell violence" when they hear the phrase "liberation theology", which they associate with ruinously revolutionary ideologies that maintained the Communist Block in Eastern Europe. Even the brilliant and one of my much admired theologians Tina Beattie describes Latin American liberation theology (which is what has allegedly spread throughout the world, according to her) as "an attempt at a synthesis between Catholic Theology and Marxism".[68] It was this same misleading over-simplification

---

[67] See "What Religions Have to Say about Freedom, Justice and Human Rights" (Editorial), *Dialogue NS*, xxxv-xxxvi (2008-2009), pp.i-iv.
[68] T. Beattie, *The New Atheists: The Twilight of Reason and War on Religion*, Darton, Longman, Todd, London, 2007 (reprint 2008), p. 31.

that seemed to have prompted Cardinal Ratzinger's well-known warnings about this theology. A clarification is needed here:-

Liberation theology is not really a Marxist reading of the Bible, though there have been such attempts on the part of certain individuals such as Jose Miranda. If there are some points of agreement between Marxist and biblical teachings, as for instance, (a) the repudiation of any slavery-based economy that allows a leisure class to live at the expense of a worker-class, (b) the necessity of freedom struggles on the part of the exploited (as it happened in Egypt) or (c) the dream of an egalitarian society (as experimented by the Jews on their arrival in Canaan *(Judges)* and later also by the earliest Christian communities *(Acts),* then the only sane conclusion to be drawn is that *the Bible could not have copied it from Marx* who came centuries later. It should be the other way about.

I grant, however, that there was some basis for that misapprehension. First, the tools of social analysis associated with Marxism were certainly resorted to by many of us to diagnose the roots of societal inequalities just as the Freudian tools of psychoanalysis have served Christian medical persons for diagnosing mental disorder. Secondly, the EATWOT appeared to be the Christian counterpart of the Non-Align movement, whose Nation Members, in opposing the Capitalism of the West, were naturally leaning towards the Eastern/Marxists Block; so, too, some Third World Theologians of the EATWOT, motivated by the same reason, were critically sympathetic towards the Socialist experiment of East European countries —though this experiment was not exactly socialism but a species of state-capitalism! But the negligibly few Christian militants who brandished the picture of Christ holding a gun, specially in Latin America, were *not* represented in the EATWOT and were a passing fad.

101

The truth of the matter is that "Liberation Theology" in Latin America as well as in Asia is the direct result of a *lectio divina* made by theologians in the company of the poor and the powerless.[69] There was no place in it for violence or even counter-violence of any kind! Christianity, as a religion of love advocating debt-cancellation, forgiveness and reconciliation, constitutes the content and the essence of all liberation theologies.

In Chapter VII, I deal with some of the Western writers who have misrepresented our position regarding this issue. All that we wish to assert, here, is that even "counter-violence" is not entertained in any Asian Liberation theology worth its name, while on my part, I can *understand* people resorting to that solution but I cannot *justify* that option. For instance, in our country, it is the successive Sinhala Governments' racial-linguistic discrimination and various forms of violence that provoked the Tamils to take to counter-violence. But peace was not won through that means. Some Tamil theologians had appealed to Samson's example in *Judges* to justify suicide-bombing that killed many innocents. This kind of biblical literalism is a dangerous game to play. Not everything recorded in the Scripture is the Word of God, as we have argued in Part One! We agree with the recent popes that, given the weapons of mass destruction used today, no war could be deemed just. In fact, here in our country, the ethnic war has not ended, and violence is deeply imbedded in the minds of the new generation.

On the other hand we must follow the divine strategy employed both in the Old and the New Testaments:- urgent appeals disregarded by the oppressors should, at some stage,

---

[69] "Jon Sobrino and Liberation Theology" *VJTR*, Vol 17/8R, August 2007, pp. 626-28; "Jon Sobrino und die Theologie der Befreiung" *Forum Welt-Kirche*, July August 2007, pp.31-32. See the Internet for French and Spanish versions.

assume a **non-violence that hurts** their pride. Gandhi's non-violence became effective only when it irritated the oppressor. It was a principle followed by Jesus and the Jewish prophets. Jesus was not at loggerheads with the Jews or critical of the God of the Old testament as if YHWH were an unmerciful tyrant; what Jesus countered was the contemporary religious leaders' interpretations of the OT and of the God revealed therein —when such interpretations condoned injustice. The Romans were not the immediate oppressors, as were certainly the high priests and their colleagues who used that colonial power of Rome to their own advantage (as clearly illustrated in the way Jesus' assassination was engineered); these religious leaders (not the Jews as such, nor all the Pharisees either) were the target of Jesus' smarting vituperations. Where non-violent communication fails, a more confrontational language needs to be resorted to. This is the prophetic tradition that Jesus adopted as a faithful Jew. As one who had opted to be poor —no place to be born in, to lay his head on or even to be buried in— he also opted for the oppressed by *openly associating with them, becoming their friend as well as their voice and indulging in a deliberately provocative violation of all the human-made discriminatory laws that marginalized them.* It was love that forced him to risk the fatal consequences of that option. Prophetic anger is an expression of love; for anger is not hatred, as I have explained to my non-Christian collaborators, and even more to our Western Critics.[70] This is the policy that guides liberation theologians in Asia.

This policy, let me re-iterate, includes the aforementioned obligation to bridge the language barrier with the non-Christian majority whose *religious idiom* together with its

---

[70] See Chapter VII and also "What *on Earth* is God doing with us? A Recovery of Authentic Christian Theism", *Gleanings*, XXVII / 1 & 2 (January-June 2008), 3-16.

liberative content needs to be mastered by the Asian theologians not only doctrinally or theoretically but also —as far as possible— experientially and practically even if it means, in special circumstances, *per communicationem in sacris*. Even this enterprise is to be undertaken as far as possible with the colloboaration with *churches other than one's own*. Hence our discussion needs to be complemented and completed by a reflection on these two concerns, which will be our concluding observations of this Chapter : nos.10 (other religions) and 11 (other churches).

10. Familiarity with the "Three Moments" of *Other* Religions
Since it is the Asian religions that provide the church with the vernacular idiom for interpreting the Word, an Asian theologian is obliged to become familiar with the *three moments of all religions* and become even more intensely acquainted with the one that has contributed most to the formation of the culture that hosts the local church to which s/he belongs. In my case it was the insertion into Asia's multifarious religiousness that helped to read the Word within the threefold context. Honesty compels me to confess that this insertion was the result of a decision made by my superiors rather than an initiative on my part, as I have already admitted in the Introduction. The study of Indology in general and Buddhism in particular —a mission given to me by my superiors— was a great grace. Whereas Hinduism is mostly an *Indic* religion, albeit with a universal message, Buddhism is a *pan-Asian* religion that has shaped the minds and hearts of about twenty political enclaves in Asia, perhaps just little more than Islam (though perhaps the latter is numerically stronger than the former). Many an Asian theologian is summoned to delve into Buddhism since it has shaped the cultures of Western, Southern, South Eastern, Far-Eastern and Central regions of Asia.

On the other hand one cannot study Theravada Buddhism without a *thorough* study of every branch of Hinduism, though the study of Hinduism does not necessarily entail a specialization in Buddhism. Thus I was academically compelled to go deep into the Vedic texts, the Six Classical Systems of Indic Philosophy, and particularly the Vedanta, not to mention Jainism. This entry into Indic Religiosity, even its popular forms (as explained in the next Chapter), was further helped by my nearly seven-year sojourn in India. Thus my specialization in Theravada Buddhism made me plunge into every dimension of what goes under the name of 'Hinduism' and also Jainism. During my Tertianship in Ahamadabad, my Tertian Instructor, Fr Conget, gave me permission to continue my research in Jain-Buddhist controversies in the Jain Institute that was only walking distance from Newman House where I lived. My Buddhist studies put me in contact with three major Indic religions and their philosophies. This, I realized, was an indispensable requirement for a South Asian who wants to theologize.

As a professor of Buddhism I was also obliged to study and teach also the *other forms of Asian Buddhism*. In fact it was I who introduced to the Gregorian University's curriculum a course on *Buddismo come Fenomeno Contemporaneo* in 1972, in place of theoretical Buddhism taught there up to then by my predecessor(s). I spent a few months in London University's SOAS (School of Oriental and African Studies) to update and perfect my knowledge of doctrinal ramifications as well as the historical manifestations of each branch of Buddhism before I taught that course. I also visited as many countries as possible, where Buddhism was either the predominant religion or at least a socially significant phenomenon, and did some field work after a preliminary study of that country's Buddhism. I visited, Nepal, Myanmar (Burma), Thailand, Malaysia, Hong Kong, Singapore, S. Korea and Japan. I also studied and taught the history and character of Buddhism in those countries that I could not visit. [71]

In order to acquire a good grasp of the role played by this religion in those culturally diversified regions, I committed myself to an intense study the *national history* of each political territory in Asia (South, South East, Central and Far East) where Buddhism is the official or the major religion. Such a study forced me to delve into other *non-Buddhist religions* that influenced Asian cultures (such as Islam, Shinto, Daoism and Confucianism) and study the socio-political and economic basis of each country. One could not be a teacher of Buddhism without this kind of extensive and comprehensive on-going study, which was as engaging as it was enjoyable. The spiritual opulence of our continent is staggering, and I was overwhelmed by this discovery!

On the other hand I realized very soon in the course of my Asian pilgrimage that the Asians who profess any one of three **Abrahamic religions** —Judaism, Christianity or Islam— cannot be faithful to   God revealed in their respective scriptures without sincerely seeking to know the *divine purpose* of allowing the rise of non-Abrahamic (or *gnostic* religions), both Indic and Sinic. Such faithfulness to God requires that the followers of these three *agapeic* religions of Semitic provenance come together and think together on this phenomenon instead of indulging in an internecine hostility and fratricide. I had only a glimpse into the Jewish-Muslim conflict during my visit to the Holy Land in 1966, crossing from the Jewish sector to the Muslim sector in Jerusalem. An unpleasant experience of being suspected as a Pakistani spy at Kusinar (during the height of the Indo-

---

[71] I entered Vietnam in 1973, but at the Air Port the Van Thieu Government refused a visa alleging that I was a Marxist hailing from a Marxist country for they had interrupted my correspondence with some Vietnamese regarding the phenomenon of Buddhist monks staging political protests through self-immolation.

Pakistan War) gave me a taste into how Muslims are viewed by some Hindus! Add to this the Muslim-Christian conflicts flaring up in most parts of the globe. The rifts and rivalries among them prevent both parties from focusing together on the gift they are called by Providence to share with the adherents of non-Semitic religions on vital issues such as the value of matter and marriage, the soteriological purpose of present existence and, of course, eschatology.[72]

My interest in Judaism was kindled by my study of Hebrew and was maintained by the bible-study sessions I have been conducting for various groups of Christians for nearly four decades. That is why I said in the Introduction that an Asian theologian has to be a Semite in spirit! I regret my insertion into Islam was not as deep as with other major religions, though I took every possible step in my power to acquaint myself with the Holy Koran and other works on Islam's history, doctrine and practice. I also proposed the name of a Jesuit confere who could specialize on Christian-Muslim Dialogue and join our Centre to complement my work; this dream could not be realized as the superiors did not pursue my plan, though for Hinduism we have a resource person in Fr Roy Fernando, my successor in Tulana.

Yet in the seminars on inter-religious encounter for inter-ethnic reconciliation conducted at Tulana thanks to the sponsorship of the Peace and Justice desk of the Methodist Church in Sri Lanka, many exemplary Muslim clerics and scholars have honoured us with their participation and enhanced my knowledge of their religion which, of course, I

---

[72] For a more detailed discussion see "The Holy Spirit and Asia's Religiousness", *Spiritus, A Journal of Christian Spirituality* (John Hopkins University Press), VII/2 (Fall 2007), pp. 138-139. [The original version appeared in Italian : "Lo Spirito Santo e L'Asia", (eds. M.Amaladoss & R.Gibellini), *Theologia in Asia*, Queriniana, Brescia, 2006, 383-410]; the English version has been reprinted in *Third Millennium*, Vol IX No 3, July-September 2006, pp. 08-27 and in *Asian Christian Review* (Japan), Vol 1, No 3 (December 2007), pp. 51-66.

had already encountered in the class-rooms and the play-ground as a teenage student of St Aloysius College, which educated most of the Muslim males in the city of Galle. A Christian Indologist loses his or her perspective on the Asian reality if he or she neglects the study of Islam. In fact I am pleased that in the Centre for the Education of Hearing Impaired Children (CEHIC), founded and run by Sr Greta Nalawatta with the close collaboration with our Tulana Centre, we have Muslims and Hindus who maintain their identity while being integrated into a community that is mostly Christian and Buddhist. One of the five principles of education practiced there is inter-religious harmony and cooperation.[73]

The current wave of aggressively fundamentalist forms of religion (both Hindu, Buddhist, Christian and Muslim) has also been taken into account in our study and encounter sessions with the help of activists who are engaged in peace and reconciliation in various parts of our country, while closely monitoring similar events in other parts of Asia. As noted in many of my previous writings, a religion becomes aggressive when it is subservient to an ideology, e.g. nationalism, which might have initially served adherents of a religion for a legitimate purpose (say, anti-Colonial struggle for Independence as it happened in many Asian countries) but would outlive its purpose and begin to distort the original liberative essence of that religion; there are also other *ideologies* (e.g. racism, sexism etc) which are incompatible with any religion and which, therefore, make religionists irreligious.[74] Our task is to engage in an inter-religious dialogue that would gently expose such ideological contaminations.

---

[73] See "Five Principles of a Humanistic Education: Lessons Learnt from a Thirty year Experiment", *Dialogue NS*, vol. xxxix (2012) pp. 107-120.
[74] E.g., *ATL*, pp. 24-31.

11. Ecumenical Approach to Inter-religious Collaboration in Theopraxis

I coined the two terms *"inter-ecclesial* ecumenism" and *"trans-ecclesial* ecumenism" in the early 1970s,[75] because my attempt to see an Asian Theology evolving from a reading of the Word in the context of Asia's religiousness and poverty was essentially an *ecumenical* one but not in the traditional sense of ecumenism, which is one of various churches talking to each other about their differences and similarities in order to reach some doctrinal consensus, as in the Christian Countries, and which is what I mean by *inter-ecclesial ecumenism.* Rather, ours was and is an ecumenism in which members of various churches would come out of their denominational enclaves and meet in a common arena where they join the Asians in their struggle for full humanity in the context of Asia's religiousness and social inequalities; which is what I meant by *trans-ecclesial ecumenism.* It is thanks to this second form of ecumenism that we have come to some practical agreement in such issues as *Mariology* (See Chapter II, no 6) or the debate about *faith and good works* (see Chapter II, no 8). Perhaps it was this species of *trans-ecclesial ecumenism* happening in most of the developing countries that explains the birth of the Ecumenical Association of Third World Theologians (EATWOT) in 1976.

A Vatican Nuncio questioned the canonical liceity of this species of ecumenism, insisting that in any effort to foster such ecumenism we must wait for the green light from Rome.

---

[75] In my paper "Contemporary Ecumenism and Asia's Search for Christ" presented at the Jesuits' Ecumenical Meeting in Manila in 1974, and printed in several journals: e.g., P. de Achutegui (ed.), *Towards a Dialogue of Life : Ecumenism in the Asian Context* Cardinal Bea Studies IV (Manila), 1976, *pp.* 154-74; Reprinted: *Teaching All Nations* (Manila), 13, 1976, *pp.* 23-39; *The Month,* 11(1978), *pp.* 4-9; Spanish version in: *Misiones Extranjeras* (Madrid), 31 (1976) *pp.* 14-32 ; German: *Una Sancta,* 34 (1979), *pp.* 319-32.

I gently reminded him that these divisions were not made in Asia but in Europe from where they were imported here. We cannot wait till *they* patch up *their* differences because, here, in Asia, we cannot present a dismembered body of Christ without losing our evangelical credibility and annulling our Christian witness, as has been clearly declared in the very first paragraph of *Unitatis Integratio* (Vatican II's Decree on Ecumenism).

This species of thinking and activity cutting across churches led me to the conclusion that *every form of inter-religious encounter has to happen ecumenically.* As a matter of fact, the *Asian Theology of Liberation,* here in our country, was and is the fruit of a collaborative effort of Christians, who without losing their respective denominational identities, crossed the boundaries of their own churches and acted as an undivided Christian movement joining the non-Christians in the common mission of integral liberation. For example, *Đevasarana* founded by the Anglican minister-monk Yohan Devanada, the *Christian Workers' Fellowship* (CWF) which was a creation of a politically radical ecumenical group led by Vijaya Vidyasagara, (Anglican), the Methodist Church's *Centre for Religion and Society* (CRS) founded by Rev. Basil Jackson and later restructured by Rev. Lynn de Silva as the *Ecumenical Institute for Study and Dialogue* (EISD), Tissa Balsuriya's *Centre for Society and Religion* (CSR), *Satyodaya* co-founded by the Jesuit Paul Caspersz and Bishop Leo Nanayakkara, and *Tulana* which I founded as well as Mervyn Fernando's *Subodhi* —**were all various apostolic enterprises that collaborated *trans-ecclesially* in responding to the Asian reality of religiousness and poverty.**[76]

---

[76] Various examples of "formal" and "informal" *trans-ecclesial ecumenism,* as practiced in Sri Lanka and their characteristics as well as by-products together with six observations about them can be read in my paper "Ecumenism and Inter-faith Relationship: The Sri Lankan Experience", a talk given at the international

Summary and Conclusion: My exposure to **all** *metacosmic* religions, with various degrees of intensity together with my close study and experience of their "popular forms" as well as of various *cosmic* religions (tribal, Dalit, shamanistic etc) through both desk-work and field-work —more about it in Chapter IV below— made me **discover** that in the Asian Reality as a whole there is *an implicit urge for holistic liberation,* which I strove to make explicit and to articulate theologically within the biblical perspectives described in Part One. Thus **an Asian theology is** *discovered* **and** *not invented.* I am embarrassed when some speak of "Aloysius Pieris's Theology" as if it were a new creation of mine. For my sole contribution was that of *reading* God's Word in the context of Asia's manifold religiousness and scandalous poverty with my ear tuned to the voice that I am accustomed to *hear* in the Hebrew and Christian Scriptures, which I continue to read and study incessantly *in consultation and collaboration with colleagues from other Christian Churches.* It is this methodology that I recommend in these pages to young Asian theologians.[]

ecumenical conference held to celebrate the bicentenary of the National Christian Conference, 20th July, 2013 at Meth Arana, Aturugiriya, Sri Lanka and to be published by the NCC in the near future.

CHAPTER IV
My Discovery of Cosmic Religiosity
AS AN INDISPENSABLE INGREDIENT OF AN
ASIAN LIBERATION THEOLOGY AND ITS MISSIOLOGY

1. Discovering the Hindu and Catholic Versions

I may have encountered this species of religiosity in the
people of my country since childhood, but I could not have
recognized and named it as what I *today* know it to be. I was
almost 25 years old when I consciously chanced upon it for
the first time and it was in connection with Hinduism. The
"Hinduism" we were taught at the Jesuit Faculty of
Philosophy (Sacred Heart College, Shambaganur, India)
consisted of the classical six systems of Indian philosophy
and a module on the three medieval thinkers Shankhara,
Madhava and Ramanuja. There was also a course on the
Bhagavadgīta, interpreted as a philosophical synthesis of the
three paths (*mārgas*) : the affective way (*bhakti-mārga*), the
active way (*karma-mārga*) and the sapiential way (*jñāna-
mārga*). They were transcendental systems of thought, which
I would name "metacosmic" a couple of decades later —
though the *bhakti* tradition (sometimes combined with *karma*
tradition) was easily absorbed by the lower classes in
medieval India as a vehicle of liberation from class and
gender oppression.[77] This was particularly true of Mahatma
Gandhi's Ashram and his movement in the 20th century. This
tradition continues.

---

[77] See *ATL*, pp. 103-104.

The discovery of *the other* species of Hinduism occurred when, after finishing my studies in philosophy in April 1959, I went to Madras (modern Chennai) to learn the Sanskrit language under the private tutorship of Prof. Dr V. Varadachari. While studying the Poet Kalidasa's epic poem *Kumārasambhava* under his guidance, I was intrigued by the underlying belief that God Shiva —in conformity with the will of the Supreme Divinity (*Maghavān*)— interrupted his ascetical practices after being seduced by Cupid (*Ananga*) to court and copulate with Pārvatī for the divine purpose of bringing forth the Child-Saviour (*Kumāra*) who was to deliver the world from evil. This species of soteriology was shockingly alien to my scholastic mentality and Dr Varadachari explained to me that Kalidasa put into verse a story drawn from the **more** *popular* **stream of Hinduism** promoted in the ***Purāṇa*** literature which was as validly Hindu as the content of speculative philosophies. In compliance with his advice I made use of my sojourn in Chennai to personally observe this species of "Puranic Hinduism" as practised in many of the temples that adorned that city. That was my initiation into what I would *later* call "cosmic religiosity".

The Roman Catholic version of this religiosity came my way when I was in Naples for my theological studies a few years later. Our professor of Sociology, Paolo Tufari, a Harvard trained social scientist, took four of us, Jesuit theology students, to the Marian Shrine at Sacromonte, in Vallo di Lucania in southern Italy, to make a sociological study of Christianity practised by the ordinary people. It was just after my ordination, at the end of the third year of theology. Tufari educated us to adopt a positive posture towards this phenomenon; and that helped me in my pastoral activities there, both in the confessional and outside; I became more sensitive and sympathetic towards the belief-practice cycle that I observed among the pilgrims who came from the

113

remotest villages of the *campagna* (the rural interior). It was the faith of Italy's rural poor expressed in terms of their *this-worldly* needs: money, marriage, family, food, health and happiness, which were as important a part of Christian faith as the officially promoted zeal for "saving one's soul" by attaining a supposedly *other-worldly* goal. Thanks to this experience, I began my fourth year of theology as a presbyter equipped with a positive and constructive approach in my extensive apostolate among the suburban people in Pozzuoli as well as the less privileged citizens of Naples in Rione di Traiano and among the sick in the hospital (Clinica Mediterranea) as mentioned earlier. Thanks to Paolo Tufari, the Jesuit Sociologist, I learnt to appreciate the *people's spirituality*, which began to evoke in me the cries of the poor heard in the psalms addressed to YHWH whom such people found in their company as their Immanuel. I sensed a *biblical* resonance in their *earthly* approach to Christian faith.

2. Research into the Buddhist Version of Cosmic Religiousness

The two aforementioned encounters with the popular *this-worldly* religiosity —the one in Chennai in a Hindu context (1959) and the other in the Christian ethos of southern Italy (1965)— had already whetted my curiosity about the Buddhist version of this species of spirituality. As I began my doctoral studies in Buddhism in Sri Lanka immediately after my return from my theological studies in Naples (1966 onwards), I began to probe into this area as a side-interest while my doctoral research revolved mostly around the philosophical teachings deposited in the Pali exegetical literature. As advised by my thesis director, Ven. Dr K. Wachissara Thera (Buddhist Monk and Scholar), I visited many Buddhist temples in the island, living as a layman, for I was warned that if I were to present myself in my clerical garb, the attention given to me as an honoured guest would reduce the freedom I needed to observe and learn from a

114

firsthand experience of contemporary Buddhism. Also during this period of doctoral studies (1967-1971), I worked among the poor in the urban slums of Dematagoda (Colombo) where it was popular Hinduism and popular Buddhism that converged in the lives of the urban destitute class, and where I also noticed a conspicuous absence of ethnic tensions. I was getting more and more fascinated by the contrast between the Buddhism I was studying for my doctorate and the beliefs and practices of the masses.

By that time I had struck a deep friendship with Rev. Dr Lynn A. de Silva of the Methodist Church, whom I joined in a *trans-ecclesially* ecumenical venture of facing the Buddhist reality together as a common Christian enterprise (see pp.109-111). I discussed this matter of popular religiosity with him on many occasions because he too had been intrigued by this same phenomenon. Eventually he wrote a book on it —the first of its kind— which I read carefully in compliance with his request and suggested for it the title *Buddhism: Beliefs and Practices.* At that period of time I had not yet coined the term "Cosmic Religiosity of the Buddhists", which could have been the appropriate title for that book.

After my doctoral studies, I spent more quality-time on this aspect of Buddhism, visiting various parts of the island practising what anthropologists used to call "participatory observation". Healing ceremonies both in the Hindu Shrine at Kataragama frequented by masses of Buddhists and other such sites in other parts of the country attracted my attention because of their *cosmicity.*[78] Gradually I came to call this phenomenon "cosmic religiosity" in contrast with the "metacosmic religion" that I had doctored myself in. I also visited various parts of the Island, spending a few days in

---

[78] For one such study, see *Prophetic Humour*, pp. 25-40.

115

each place, studying the people and their *mores*. A few days in Akkaraipattu and specially Arugambay (1980s) in the Eastern Coast allowed me to see fishermen representing all religions and languages in the country assembling together at a particular season. I camped out in both Tamil and Sinhala areas and shared their lives. Their Buddhism and Hinduism were preponderantly cosmic.

3. The Legitimization of the Term "Cosmic"

The reason for the choice of this term was to distinguish the "*religious* this-worldliness" of popular Buddhism from the "*non-religious* this-worldliness" that the term "secular" indicates in the West. The Greek *kosmos* and the Latin *saeculum* means the world, but since the expression *secular* is already in use as a synonym for non-religious this-worldliness, I coined the term "cosmic" to convey the Asian form of this-worldliness which is profoundly religious. Thus I distinguished it not only from the "secularity" of the West's technoctatic culture spreading into Asia but equally from the "spirituality" of the major religions that postulate a "metacosmic (not acosmic) horizon" as the *Summum Bonum*.

By this time my usual passion for historical studies (see pp.59-63) had led me to a survey of various *revolutionary struggles and social contestations* recorded in the political history of Asia and I discovered to my pleasant surprise that *in general* most of these anti-establishment postures were initiated by the social stratum inspired by a cosmic religiosity, whereas the protagonists of the metacosmic religions *on the whole* were tilting towards the establishment. This discovery made me realize that a liberation theology — a theology that is not a liberation theology is not theology— cannot distance itself from cosmic religiosity of the poor. I brought this out in my paper read at the first Asian Theological Consultation of the EATWOT at Wennappuwa in 1979, the same paper where I proposed the "poverty-religiosity" paradigm as a substitute for the more common "inculturation-liberation" scheme which I banished from the theological discourse as misleading.

Quite understandably, a couple of South Asian theologians were initially critical of my demand for a shift from the Inculturation-Liberation paradigm to religiousness-poverty paradigm, as well as my insistence on the role of *cosmic religiosity* in the discovery of an Asian Theology, probably because *at that time*, they were busy 'inculturating' Christian thought in the metacosmic religiosity associated with Vedantic philosophy, thus replicating the West's traditional scholastic theology which employed Greek philosophies as its framework. This effort was accompanied by a species of Brahmanization, which is most evident in the Indian Rite Mass and which did not resonate with Puranic Hinduism of the masses and the cosmic spirituality of the Tribals and the Dalits. It sounds strange but it is also true that mine was the first paper that dealt *formally* with the Dalits and Tribals at EATWOT and that was in Delhi in 1981.

The prejudice against primal cultures that practice a *cosmic religiosity*, is rooted in the widespread misconception that they are "primitive", "barbaric", "superstitious" and 'pre-historical" because they are allegedly stuck at a *stage that preceded modern civilization.* The delusion of the so-called moderns, as O'Murchu has argued, is that "civilization" took place 7000 (seven thousand) years ago with the dawn **urbanization** in the Middle East (evolution of the first *cities* in the area occupied by modern Syria, Israel and Palestine) and **literacy** (development of *writing* once again in the Middle East (in the Sumerian culture) and that whatever preceded these two events was "pre-history" [79], when the

---

[79] D.O'Murchu, *God in the Midst of Change: Wisdom for Confusing Times,* Claretian Publications, Quezon City, 2012, pp.12-17.

so-called illiterate primitives are alleged to have lived as carnivorous savages; but recent research has shown that "prior to five thousand years ago (out of an evolutionary story of seven million years) there is scant evidence for the myth of the hunting male. For most of our time, we were horticultural food-gatherers rather than meat hunters".[80] Hence *cosmic religiosity* that has survived the so-called *civilization* to tell this story to our own globally messed-up generation, summons us to an environmentally human and socially cohesive life-style, in short, back to a civilization that we have foolishly abandoned as primitive!

I was pleasantly surprised to notice that this terminology as well as the reality that my neologism "cosmic religiosity" describes has entered Rome's magisterial teaching thanks to Marcello Zago, omi and Jacques Dupuis sj, who drafted John Paul II's encyclical *Redemptoris Missio,* not to mention the FABC teachings which, too, have adopted these concepts quite freely, thanks again to the theologians who drafted them. They are now part and parcel of the *official* Catholic Theological vocabulary!

But I wonder whether the Papal Magisterium has ever realized that its understanding of Asian religiosity in terms of the cosmic-metacosmic differentiation as advocated in *Redemptoris Missio* could forebode serious consequences for the official missiology advocated by that same Magisterium! In fact my *Concilium* article "Has Christ a Place in Asia?",[81] where I spelt out this missiology, was countered with a platitudinous restatement of the old mission theology rather than with a rationally argued response in *Avvenire d'Italia,* the official organ of the Italian Episcopate!(1993) When my friend Prof. Rossino Gibellini sent me a photocopy of this

---

[80] *Ibid.* p. 34, supported by Robert Sussman and Donna Hart, *Man the Hunted,* (2005).
[81] *Concilium,* 1993/2, 33-47.

article asking me whether I would like to send a rebuttal, I replied that any reply on my part to that article would be as futile and ludicrous as the effort to "wake up someone who is feigning to sleep", as we say in our native tongue! Here below is a brief summary of my thesis.

4. Missiological Consequences of Understanding Religiosity as "Cosmic" and "Metacosmic"
I have been often confronted by Fundamentalist Christians and radical evangelicals in the mainstream churches citing Chapter Two of *The Acts* in support of their thesis that the mission mandate of Jesus was literally carried out by the nascent church through *mass conversions* in the Mediterranean basin and that it constitutes a *Scripturally revealed obligation* of the church at all places and at all times.

I always quote back to them the power of binding and losing which Jesus gave *The Twelve*, who represented the New Israel, or the nuclear church. The way they used that power in Acts Chapter 15 should also guide our response to the Missionary Mandate given by the Risen Lord. The Apostles decided together with their Mission Partner, the Holy Spirit ("it seemed good to us and the Holy Spirit") to dispense the gentile neo-converts with the *divinely* revealed and *divinely* imposed law of circumcision. What authority did they have to make such a drastic change on a practice that the scriptures upheld as a sacrosanct injunction of God?

The answer is that Jesus Christ did not leave a book of instruction or a *Codex Juris Canonici* to guide the church; instead, he breathed into us his own Holy Spirit as the internal teacher, personal guide and the church's "mission-companion". For **both the Holy Spirit** (through whom the Risen Lord abides and works within us) **and we, the Church**

119

were co-sent by Christ as collaborators in his mission.[82] In their decision about the law of circumcision, they and the Spirit were responding together to the signs of the times. They arrived at a new mission theology, i.e., a new interpretation of the Word in the context of the Asian reality. For as we explained in Part I, the history of Israel was given as a sample of how God works through any people's history so that we (the church) can learn to hear, recognize and obey that same voice in contemporary events. As the nascent church did at the Council of Jerusalem, we who are heirs to that same tradition should listen to what the same Lord speaks in today's Asian context and respond to Her summons. The Spirit inspires us with a *new understanding* of Christ's Mission Mandate as dictated by the signs of the times.

To put it differently, the Asian context reveals the need for a missiological method very different from the one that the social context of the Roman Empire demanded of the first century Christians. That was an era when the Imperial Rome was in decline and its Greco-Roman religions were on the wane, thus creating a spiritual vacuum in the cultures that were once dominated by that religiosity. Christianity, by Providential design, was summoned to fill that gap. But in Asia the context is diametrically different. Here the Asian religions are asserting themselves more zealously than ever before and challenging the Westernized Christianity that is imported here but abandoned in the West. What inhibits our new missiological initiatives here in Asia is that this same 'failed Christianity' of the Western Patriarchate is held out as the criterion of orthodoxy for Asian churches, as mentioned earlier. Furthermore, the Prosperity Gospel imported from the rich countries by a handful of fundamentalist Christians

---

[82] Y. Congar, *The Mystery of the Church*, Geoffrey Chapman, London, 1965, pp.105; 119.

have disrupted national peace and inter-church harmony in many parts of Asia.

Against this series of events we must also study the sociological data that reveal the mind of God and pay attention to what I call the "Helicopter Theory of Religious Expansion".[83] History of the spread of metacosmic religions such as Hinduism, Buddhism, Christianity and Islam in Asia indicate that the *cosmic religions* had served as the 'helicopter-pad' on which the *metacosmic* religions had "landed", so to say. Where one helicopter (i.e., a metacosmic religion), has alighted on a landing pad (i.e., cosmic religiosity), another cannot. This explains why Christianity swept through the Philippines during the same centuries in which a similar form of colonial Christianity failed to convert India, Sri Lanka and other countries where already Buddhism or Hinduism had arrived earlier and sunk their roots in the cultures permeated by cosmic religions.

Today, on the other hand, mass conversion to Christianity is evidenced only in places where cosmic religions of tribal cultures prevail, such as Oceania and in certain parts of Asian countries. Shinto and Confucianism are refined, elegant and cultivated expressions of cosmic religiosity that has served as the pad for Buddhism to land on in Japan and China respectively. But where Buddhism is itself more Confucianist or cosmic, mass conversion to Christianity seems evident. Where Confucianism dominates, as for instance, in Korea and China, conversion to Christianity is less difficult. Only individual conversions are recorded in other areas. This is the general pattern observed in the expansion of various religions in Asia.

---

[83] *Concilium, art.cit.*; reprinted in *Fire and Water, pp.*65-78 .

Obviously demographic changes through immigrants belonging to one religion infiltrating into such cultures can gradually push the helicopter aside! Forceful replacement is not ruled out. But that is not an option allowed to Jesus-followers. The fact that Asia has remained non-Christian after two millennia of our missionary presence, gives us a message that we should reflect over seriously. God seems to reveal through these historic-sociological data *another way* of preaching the gospel and *another way* of understanding "conversion".[84]

5. Post-Vatican II Missiology
The foregoing considerations force upon us a new understanding of other religions as well as a new notion of 'conversion'. Way back in 1969, I had presented the way the church evolved its theology of religions in *four steps* beginning with the 16th century.[85] There I had indicated how each new step was an improvement on the previous one, thus showing a certain progress in the way the church understood the church and non-Christians vis-à-vis the Reign of God. Here below is a summary of that presentation

The first two theories identified the Church with God's Reign (God's Reign being another name for Christ as the plenitude of Revelation and Salvation, as explained in Chapter II above). This false equation gave birth to the missiological principle, "no salvation outside the church" and "no revelation outside the bible". In other words, no other religion can offer redemption to humankind and no other

---

[84] For an extensive discussion on this new missiology, see "Two Mission Mandates Calling for Conversion: *Preach the Dhamma* (Vin. I:21) and *Proclaim the Gospel* (Mk 16:15)", *Dialogue NS*, vols. xxxii-xxxiii (2005-2006) pp. 1-57.

[85] "Church, Kingdom and the Other Religions", *Dialogue (OS)*, No. 22, October 1970, 3-7, a printed version of the address given at the Anglican Synod of Kurunegala in 1969. Fr Jean Leclerq, osb, the well-known medievalist made and circulated a French translation of it for the perusal of francophone monastics around 1974.

religious book contains the salvific truth. Pope Gregory VII, went as far as to say that the non-Christians cannot be saved unless they are juridically subjected to papal authority which, according to another Pope, Innocent IV, consists of the papal possession of the salvific power that Christ himself wields over the whole of creation. In the 16th century the church's aggressive rejection of the previously known non-Christian religions, Judaism and Islam, formed the social background of its theology of religion.[86] Thus another Pope, St Nicholas V conferred on the European Colonizers the "full and free permission to invade, search out, capture and subjugate the Saracens, the pagans and *other enemies of Christ"*. All other religions were **ANTI-CHRISTIAN** (enemies of Christ) and the other religionists had to be *conquered* for Christ. I called it the **conquest theory**

The Jesuit of the 16th century redeemed us of this ecclesiastical imperialism (or the "conquest theory") by suggesting that though the *religions* are outside the pale of redemption, the *cultures* in which such religions express themselves are a *neutral area* where the seed of salvation (which is Christianity) can be sown. De Nobili converted many Brahmans in South India and Ricci many members of the Cultural elite in China because these converts did not have to give up their *cultural* practices on entering the church. Christianity replaced other religions in a cultural matrix created by those same religions. But the identification of the Church with God's Reign was taken for granted. Other religions were not exactly anti-Christian as in the previous era, but merely **NON-CHRISTIAN**. It was known then as the **adaptation theory** (or inculturation theory in modern parlance). A step forward, no doubt.

---

[86] *Give Vatican II a Chance,* pp. 152-155.

123

The breakthrough (the third model) came in the Catholic church thanks to those (like the Belgian Jesuits in Calcutta) who proposed that all these religions can be seen to be within the salvific Rule of God on the analogy of Israel which, it was claimed, came to completion in Christ and became the Church, the New Israel. All non-Christian religions, it was thought, began as part of God's Reign awaiting *fulfillment* in Christianity. This is what Vatican II was ready to accept. Most Asians were not very happy with this rather condescending approach to other religions. According to this view, other religions are neither anti-Christian, nor non-Christian but **PRE-CHRISTIAN** awaiting to be fulfilled in the Church. I called this the **fulfillment theory** in my 1969 discourse.

Karl Rahner, therefore, came up with a far-reaching insight, which constitutes the fourth paradigm. Unfortunately he employed an offensive appellation for non-Christian Religiousness: He named other religionists **ANONYMOUS CHRISTIANS**. But I have reformulated his proposal in a way that clearly coincides with his own ecclesiology, calling it the **Sacramental Theory:-**

The universal church has become a massive monolith, not small enough to be a sign of God's Reign; rather, the church must become a communion of *little flocks of Christ*, scattered among the various other religions and humanistic ideologies which, too, would be so many [anonymous] "expressions of God's Reign". A local church's function is to be *a sacrament of salvation* in each locality where it is placed by Providence. This implies that every church should *assimilate* those elements of God's Reign that are found in the non-Christian environment in which it grows, as if to say, with Vatican II, that "we Christians *acknowledge, conserve and foster* these salvific features which you non-Christians have preserved for humankind", e.g. monasticism and the meditation tradition of

124

Asia. At the same time the church has to distance itself in its praxis from those elements in other religions that are clearly anti-Kingdom, such as the caste system or certain dubious forms of sacrifices. Such a church would be a local "sign and instrument" of Salvation —salvation as revealed also in the non-Christian religions and cultures. Thus the universal church would be a communion of *locally diversified* communities of Christians, each community witnessing to Christ and appropriating the gifts of Salvation characteristic of other religions in each respective locality.

One of the corollaries of this missiology is that there are two distinct vocations. One is the **universal vocation to** *what we Christians call* **'God's Reign'** (even in its non-Christian manifestations); *all are called to it, in the sense that salvation is offered to all.* The second vocation is the **call to membership in one particular religious group which serves as a visible sign and a practical path of salvation; the call to enter the church is one such vocation,** in the sense that one may be called to witness to Christ in a church that has so assimilated the non-Christian expressions of the Kingdom as to become a **"Sacrament [**i.e., a recognizable *sign* and encouraging *means*] **of Salvation"** to the non-Christians of that particular locality. Other religions, too, are such signs and paths of salvation —salvation understood as the liberation of the rich from the lure of riches, the poor from the burden of poverty and both *classes* form their Greed, which is idolatry.

In this fourth view, evangelization does not aim at church-expansion by proselytism but amounts to the spread of the Kingdom by collaborating with other religionists in the shared responsibility for the salvation of the world. Obviously God might call someone or the other also to the church to support its vocation of being a sacrament of salvation. Such people should always be welcome into the church. There will be no inter-religious acrimony since Christianity recognizes other religions as collaborators in a common mission rather than rivals in a conversion race.

This kind of Church would enjoy the credibility necessary to share with others those elements of God's Reign which are *unique* to Christianity and which could be assimilated by other religionists without compromising their distinctiveness, just as we Christians would judiciously assimilate their unique contribution to the project of salvation without compromising our Christian identity. But the question as to what exactly constitutes Christianity's uniqueness has not received a unanimous answer. A resumé of my response to this question is offered in Chapter VII below.

6. Asian Bishops and Asian Liberation Theology

The Federation of Asian Bishops' Conferences (FABC) was established in 1972 after a valiant struggle on the part of several Asian Cardinals (Cooray, Kim, Dhramathmadja) to allay the Vatican's fears about such a venture, specially after the Vatican's misapprehension of the post-Vatican II renewal *collegially* launched by CELAM, first in Medellin (Columbia) and then in Puebla (Mexico) with its strong support for Liberation Theology.

I have always understood this theology to be Latin American Church's simultaneous response to the three inseparable emphases that marked the teachings of the Second Vatican Council, namely, (a) the autonomy of the **local churches**, (b) the centrality of **God's Word** in the life and worship and (c) the Christian responsibility for the **world's poor** —an idea that struggled hard to enter the Conciliar teachings against much resistance, thanks to Latin American participants themselves and perhaps to the emotionally charged intervention of the Franciscan Cardinal Iacome Lercaro. The Latin American Liberation theology was therefore the finest

126

fruit of Vatican II, in that the *local churches* of the most
Catholic Continent (cf. 'a' above), in obedience to *Scriptural*
teachings on justice (cf. 'b' above), responded to the cries of
their *poor* (cf. 'c'above). But there was a growing prejudice
that this theology was a mere Marxist reading of the Bible or
a sort of baptism of Marxism *a la* Thomism which was a
species of baptized Aristotelianism. The Vatican (not
excluding Paul VI) was wary of another block of Bishops in
Asia developing their own local brand of church life and
local theologies. But finally good sense prevailed and the
FABC became a reality.

The FABC's approach was quite different from that of
CELAM. Its initial intention was to concentrate on
Asianizing Christianity rather than to continue the dubious
colonial policy of *Christianizing Asia.* But the conviction that
the *cultures, religions and the poor* of Asia constituted the
context in which Asianization of churches should take place
was there in evidence since the inception of the FABC. The
mention of "cultures" and "other religions" would seem to set
Asian theology apart from the Latin American version which,
initially, laid the stress heavily and almost exclusively on the
struggle of the poor and the struggle against poverty, because
of the urgency of the need for it.

In the post-Vatican II euphoria, the Asian Theologians and
the Asian Bishops worked in harmony and that explains the
massive progress the FABC made in a host of areas that
constituted the Asian context. The FABC's inaugural address
delivered by Sri Lanka's Thomas Cardinal Cooray, which
drew the comment "Hooray for Cooray" from the Philippino
press was actually written by Sri Lanka's Tissa Balsuriya.
Since then a very well informed coterie of bishops in the
FABC joined hands with Asia's best theologians to produce
some very significant documents on missiology,
ecclesiology, spirituality, ecumenism, lay responsibility,

127

inter-religious   encounter-cum-collaboration,   social
communication and the urgent task of the emancipation of
the poor, and so on. One 'rash' act for which Jacques Dupuis
paid with his life was to proclaim loud and clear in the halls
of Rome's Gregorian University that the FABC was far
ahead of the Vatican in spelling out a theology of religions
along the Conciliar perspectives![87] His verdict was
undoubtedly true because in Asia the bishops engaged the
theologians in their search for *Asian theologies.*

The bishops and theologians who worked in the office of
human development (OHD) siphoned the contributions of
Asian thinkers into the documents of FABC. The Jesuit
Soosai Arokyasamy, Redemptorist Desmond de Souza, the
Maryknoll Father Jack Malone, and Sri Lanka's Joe
Fernando were among those working assiduously to feed the
Asian bishops with the fruit of the groundwork done by
Asian theologians. The atmosphere of mutual learning was
exemplary! I myself served as a resource person for BISA VI
and BISA VII and could not attend two more meetings to
which I was called, before health problems stopped me from
travelling altogether. Many of what we have been writing
can be recognized, sometimes *verbatim* in those FABC
documents. An entire document was dedicated to cosmic
religiosity. The Asian Liberation Theology, which is entirely
a new creation of Asia, became the official teaching of the
Episcopal Magisterium. Seeds of Liberation theology which
were sown a decade or two prior to Vatican II grew into
Dalit, Tribal, Primal, Minjung and other political theologies
in Asia,[88] and these were not dependent on the Latin

---

[87] In my last meeting with him in Rome, he mentioned casually that he made this
statement in his classes and I warned him that such statements would be taken amiss
by the Vatican if reported by outsiders who might enter his lecture room — a
warning I received from two veteran professors (Frs Flick and Alseghy) when I
began teaching in the same university.
[88] See my "Political Theologies of Asia", chapter 18 of *The Blackwell Companion
to Political Theologies,* cited above.

American version that appeared in Asia in 1971 with the publication of Gustavo Gutierrez' *Theology of Liberation* — which, no doubt, gave a boost to our theologians and to those bishops who were committed to the emancipation of the poor such as the Carmelite Labayan of Infanta in the Philippines and the Benedictine Nanayakkara of Kandy in Sri Lanka. Gutierrez is ever esteemed and appreciated in Asia.

Let it be noted that the turning point came about in 1979, at the Asian Theological Consultation (ATC) of the Ecumenical Association of Third World Theologians (EATWOT) held in Wennappuwa, Sri Lanka. Julius Cardinal Dharmaatmadja of Indonesia, Catholic Bishop Leo Nanayakkara and the Anglican Bishop Lakshman Wickramasinghe, both from Sri Lanka, represented the Asian Episcopate. Archbishop Nicolao Rotunno, the Nuncio, too made occasional appearances. Here, the Asian context which provides the framework for Asian theologies of liberation was presented by me in terms of Religiousness, *cosmic* and *metacosmic* (both in its negative and positive aspects) and Poverty (both as beatitudinal spirituality and as social misery of the masses) as explained above in detail (Chapter III, no. 6). The debate that followed this intervention of mine polarized the ATC into the *South Asian faction* (accused of promoting inculturation without liberation) and the *Hong Kong/ Philippine group* (advocating liberation based on Marxist critique of culture and religion)!

Let me repeat that my effort to avoid the inculturation-liberation paradigm did not prevent the participants from forcing "religiousness" into the inculuturation slot and "poverty" into the liberation slot! The controversy continued for two years (cf. *Voices of the Third World,* 1980) and spilt over to the Tri-continental Consultation of EATWOT in Delhi in 1981 before it was finally settled in favour of the paradigm I proposed at the ATC! The theologies that resulted from adopting this paradigm would soon permeate also the FABC documents! All is well that ends well!!!

Regrettably, it is the traditional theology of the Western Patriarchate —a hashed up neo-Thomism of the conservative branch— that is taught in many seminaries in Asia! The most creative theological output in our continent has originated, not from traditional Catholic seminaries, but from those apostolic centres where liberation praxis is combined with serious research and study.[89] This theology has not died, contrary to a biased opinion diffused by a conservative minority; it was much spoken about when it made its first appearance in Asia due to its newness; and if it is less mentioned today, it is precisely because it has come to stay as the implicit framework of contemporary Christian praxis. This is equally true of Liberation Theology in Latin America, with some Pentecostals now drawn to the biblical imperative of struggling with the poor in their effort for self-emancipation.[]

---

[89] This is true specially in Sri Lanka and the list of such Centres is given on p.110.

CHAPTER V
The Art of Communicating
an Asian Theology
THE PRIMACY OF THE OBLIQUE IDIOM

1. The Oblique Idiom and Rational Discourse

The early Latin and Greek Church Fathers employed their non-Semitic mother tongues to communicate the Word, but their mode of expression was eminently homiletic and pastoral. Thus their oral idiom guaranteed a theology that was affectively communicative unlike, say, the theology of the medieval schoolmen, whose Latin was the language of the elite and what they *wrote* was unpastorally speculative. St Ignatius recommended the former, which he called "positive theology", as an aid to one's spiritual nourishment, while appreciating "scholastic theology" *solely* for its apologetical value (Sp. Ex. 363).

The difference between the Patristic and Scholastic modes of communication lies in the affinity that the former bore to the biblical genre, on the one hand, and the discordance between the philosophical discourse of the scholastics and the oblique idiom of the Scriptures, on the other. The first lesson to be learnt from the Western Patriarchate's exaggerated resort to "reason" in theology is that the salvific '*truth*' which it tried to couch in rationally accurate verbal formulae is in fact a salvific '*event*', which can be most effectively expressed only through *evocative media of communication* such as myth and metaphor, poetry and parable, stories and symbols. It defies

131

rational discourse. Fortunately for us Asians, the First Vatican Council's "propositional" understanding of Revelation, a legacy of scholasticism, has been replaced by the Second Vatican Council's emphasis on the Self-Revelation of the Person-Event recognized as Saviour-Salvation. This step taken by this Council served the Asians as a springboard for diving into the Mystery of Salvation with head, heart and hand working in unison; i.e., with *gnosis*, *agape* and *praxis* forming an inseparable trio

I humbly submit that the *formulatory theology* that follows the unilinear logical discourse and resembles the language of mathematics may play a legitimate role in religion, but could and often did end up in irrevocable "truth-formulae" known as *dogmas*, which, in their turn lend themselves to be abused as the infallible criteria to judge a believer's faith and lead (as history has amply demonstrated) to unjust victimization of creative thinkers in the church, whereas faith, as we have insisted in many places here in this work and elsewhere, is "reliance" *('ĕmûnāh)* on God alone rather than reliance on any *creature*, including **dogmas** which are mere human constructs. [90] Hence it would seem that the Asian theologians (and Asian churches) would profit much by resorting to our time-tested tradition of the **sūtra**s which are non-dogmatic pneumonic and evocative stimuli that invite both our hearts and minds into a wide range of faith experiences accompanied by obedient action. [91]

We know that Dante Alghieri and Francesco Petrarca complement Albert, Thomas or Scotus as medieval theologians. The writings of Hildegard of Bingen of *Schivias* fame, the two Mechtilds and Gertrude and Julian of Norwich vie with those of Eckhart, Suso and Tauler as spiritualities

---

[90] See "Dogmas, Faith and God's Word: Eleven Irksome Questions for the Year of Faith (2012)" *Vagdevi* 12 (July, 2012), pp. 41-65.
[91] *Christ Beyond Dogma*, pp. 187ff.

from which theologies could be drawn out. The painter Giotto's perception of Christ and the biblical interpretations in the works of Ghiberti and Donatello are no mean theological achievements. The Baroque period produced similar *imaginative thinkers* who left their inchoative theologies in their art. For instance Bro. Andrea Pozzo, s.j., extended his influence through art beyond Europe to America and Asia where his confrères were engaged in missionary work. Michael Angelo's vision of faith and redemption demands to be studied against the background of the Reformation and the Council of Trent. And so on with other artistes.

The Catholic Bishops' Conference of India has established the *Indian Christian Artists' Forum,* because "Christian revelation and theology (*sic!*) in our country need a native expression", as has been explicitly declared in the manifesto of the CBCI Office of Social Communication. While commending this approach I would nevertheless suggest that the word "theology" be omitted from this manifesto because theology is already an interpretation. It is the artiste's interpretation of Revelation that constitutes the artiste's theology and not necessarily what another theologian imposes on him or her. For in Asia some artistes express only what they have blindly accepted from professional theologians or from church leaders. There are also others who are theologians in their own right, such as the Indian Christian artist, Jyoti Sahi, who has written theological treatises, or the Japanese novelists Ayako Miura *nee* Hotta and also Sushaku Endo, to mention some names at random. To allow such artist-theologians to emerge we must provide a space for art and sculpture, drama and film, poetry and parable, myth and metaphor, symbols and stories —in short, the "oblique idiom" resorted to in the Bible and in most other scriptural and oral traditions characteristic of Asian religions— to express what unilinear logical thinking cannot communicate. We hope that the *Asian Christian Art Association* will work along these lines. Let us also learn a lesson from the Ajantha and Ellora caves in India, which have immortalized profound facets of the Buddha's message of deliverance for generations to come; the *peasant* and the *philosopher* alike can drink from that well and be refreshed enough to start life anew.

In no way do I underestimate and much less disdain the role of reason in theology. In fact I have already mentioned above (cf. Ch. I) the academic/intellectual/ philosophical aspect of human culture as one of the three contexts for interpreting the Collective Memory for contemporary society, and not as the one and only soil in which the Word has to be sown. My *caveat* is that reason is the most deceptive and corruptible part of the human psyche. In fact in the traditional (pre-Vatican II) theology, I have discovered rational justifications of doctrines that run counter to the written and unwritten memory of the primordial slavific experience (i.e., in scripture and tradition).[92] Reason (*logos* of Greek Philosophers) is a dangerous tool in the hands of dogmatists. Our senses do not deceive us; the "deception" we attribute to them in common parlance is located in the interpretation that our *mind* gives to our sense perceptions. Our body is an innocent indicator of the effects of our mental activity. The Platonic tradition would have us believe that the mind should *exercise control over the body,* that reason should dominate senses, whereas the Buddha, who was the first known person

---

[92] E.g., the salvific necessity of Baptism for children, *logically* drawn from the Doctrine of original sin but now abandoned with Benedict XVI's declaration that there is nothing called Limbo! Also the theological arguments for an all-male presbyterium and episcopate is argued out by St Thomas on the basis of the hylomorphic theory of the Twelve Male Apostles being the "matter" and the "Do this in commemoration of me" said by Jesus at the last supper being the "form" constituting the sacrament of Orders. I discuss this in my *The Providential Timeliness of Vatican II: a Long Overdue Halt to a Scandalous Millennium?,* Kelaniya, 2013, pp. 75-83.

in history to have discovered the subconscious, knew that the mind could be deceived or manipulated by its own "reasoning" to justify what the same mind has already decided once and for all in its hidden depths. Therefore he taught his followers to *exercise control over their mind* before the mind could control the body. Furthermore, the salvific truth to be experienced "defies ratiocination" (*atakkāvacara*) and cannot be the object of rational discourse according to the much misinterpreted Kālāma Sutta of the Buddha.[93]

Our Christian *mystics* were also aware of this fact, though the non-religious world had to wait till Sigmund Freud stepped into the scene in the 19th century and came up with this important discovery. His contemporary, Karl Marx working at a sociological level had defined *ideology* as the "corruption of reason by [class] interest". Reason is corruptible in the sense that it can be self-deceptive. It is the cunning serpent of the Bible (Gen. Ch. 3), a valuable creation of God, necessary for creative behaviour and yet a "slippery" creature that needs to be handled with caution, lest it drive us to crave for a power-generating knowledge, which, we foolishly think, can make us equal to God but does in fact leave us "naked and cunning" (in Hebrew '*êrôm* and '*ārûm*) like the serpent. Reason is by nature prone to act under the impulse of self-aggrandizement or greed for power. Love which is selfless must cross-fertilize with rational knowledge to produce wisdom or discerning love (as explained in Chapter II, no. 3).

It is intriguing that the Buddha, too, differentiated the authentic doctrine of deliverance (*dhamma*) from an ideology (*diṭṭhi*), the latter amounting to a species of reasoning warped by greed or self-interest. In the best of Christian tradition, any

---

[93] See "Truth and Freedom in the Tripiṭaka and the Bible: Towards an Inter-Scriptural Dialogue" *Dialogue NS* (2008/2009), 160-180.

cognition when permeated by "non-greed" (which is what we Christians mean by *agape*, self-transcendent and other-centred love) is known as "discerning love" (*discreta caritas*), a knowing unpolluted by selfishness. Here the mind is purified and protected by selfless love which would not allow self-interest to corrupt reason. This is a common discovery of spiritual masters of both the East and the West. Hence the rectilinear reasoning process of the *logos* tradition should not only be complemented but even be corrected by the intuitional epistemology that cannot be conveyed save through the *oblique idiom* which leaves room for creative interpretations that make the original insight of a religion a source of *continuous revelation*.

This is why in our Tulana Centre, I invited non-Christian artistes to interpret Christ and Christianity in the oblique idiom. Sri Charles de Silva, a renowned Buddhist scholar and artiste complied with my request to compose a drama on the birth of Jesus, called *Raja Upatha* (The Royal Birth), after he had already created another on Christ's passion and death (*Parama Puda*), both of which I have published for the benefit of the Sinhala readership, Buddhist and Christian; his Nativity play is now available on CDs as a radio-drama with the music supplied by another famous Buddhist folk musician Rohana Baddage, and was broadcast by Sri Lanka Broadcasting Corporation a few years back as a radio play in which some of our country's very famous Buddhist artistes took part. These two texts, furthermore, have provided a new Sinhala Christian vocabulary to speak of Christ in an Asian language. The artistic license that Mr de Silva had taken in compiling these plays is as creatively faithful as that of the gospel writers (specially the author of the Fourth Gospel) have been. Similarly the mural embossments and sculptures as well as paintings in our Tulana Centre are all theological masterpieces by Buddhist artists and a source of an ever growing Asian Christology, now available on You Tube. [94]

2. Oral Transmission in the Vernacular

The Asian theology of liberation —which I did not invent but discovered within, and developed from, the socio-historical, geo-political and cultural reality of our continent— took its final shape in my mind only in and through the decades-long process of conducting *seminars in the vernacular* for Christians and Non-Christians on the Asian reality and its innate (i.e., God-given) potential for self-liberation. The encounter with the workers and workers' movements, university students, school teachers, Buddhist monks and Christian Pastors (of a wide spectrum of denominations) as well as Hindu and Muslim clergy and a host of activists working for ethnic-reconciliation and inter-human justice challenged not only me but also the adherents of all religions to read and *interpret* our respective Scriptures in terms of the primordial liberational experience which gave birth to them, as explained in Chapter I. These live exchanges which I had provoked among the participants (in the *oral idiom*) was the churning ground of the theology that I continually transpose into the *written idiom of European languages.* Let me repeat that this theology is primarily thought out and developed in an *Asian language.* It is *not* manufactured in the still politically influential foreign tongue and then translated into the vernacular (as is the case with pastoral letters of our bishops), but was thought out and *spoken* out in my native Asian tongue which is my cultural DNA.

Thus *oral transmission in the vernacular* has been a superlatively educative process for me and for the

---

[94] http://www.youtube.com/watch?feature=player_detailpage&v=0bD4xgw23nl

participants of my study-cum-encounter sessions. This policy continues to this day. Unlike the medium of writing, the oral transmission provides space for the oblique idiom which alone can convey penetrative insights that normally emerge from such encounters. Since this mode of communication had been reinforced by my own fieldwork here in our country and elsewhere in Asia (see Chapter IV above), my process of *continuous learning* from the participants of my seminars and my ongoing study of Asian history has schooled me in the art of *discerning God's Word, hearing it, acting on it, and interpreting* It, not alone but in the company of colleagues engaged in the same exercise. It involves the cooperation and the company of other Asians of all religions and no religion.

The **Basic Human Community** is the locus of such theologizing. This methodology ensures that we write from experience rather than merely write books from books; that our theology remains soteriology; that our message is tested by its ability to lead others towards the primordial experience of liberation (of each religion) as well as by its ability to recall the collective memory of that experience (written and oral/ scripture and tradition) rather than by the number of footnotes citing secondary sources. Here theology, proclamation and spirituality converge and merge. And that is what we call *Asian Theology of Liberation*

Whatever I have written for Western Readers in the rectilinear idiom of the written mode is what I have exchanged with (and learnt from) Asians in the oral idiom and in the vernacular. As a result, my writings in my own native tongue is quantitatively less compared to what I *write* in European languages. For oral communication in the vernacular allows me to use my body in a manner my computer can never do when I write my experiences down. An Asian theology has to be learnt, remembered and passed

138

on orally in the vernacular through the oblique idiom which includes body-language.[95] The gospels are written versions of oral transmissions made in the local language to the masses that spoke it [and only later transposed into Greek which was then the colonizer's (Alexander's) commercial language]; and that explains both their simplicity and depth. Such must all theology be.

3. Exploding Myths with Counter-Myths

One of the oblique idioms which we fight shy of today is 'myth'. The literal meaning of the Greek original, *mythos* (like Sanskrit *mithyā*) is 'falsehood", but its connotative sense is "truth" couched and conveyed in an oblique idiom. Transcendental truths cannot be relayed to successive generations in the exact and abstract language that smacks of mathematical formulae. Myth is the most effective medium of transmitting them. For it is a powerful way of conveying a profound truth to the subliminal regions of one's consciousness so that the mind would not only willingly accept it but even rationalize it. Myth is contrasted with history.

Let me clarify the concept of history in religious discourse. History is always an *interpretation of a chronology*, an interpretation that necessarily involves a theology or an ideology. This is true of the Bible, the Mahāvaṃsa the Chronicle of Sri Lanka, the 'history' surrounding King Arthur and the round table etc. History reads the message that chronological data hides. There is a further development

---

[95] In my study sessions for youth, specially in the decade of the eighties and early nineties, my final item used to be an exercise in theatre. I would divide the participants into small groups and give each a different theme covered in the program and invite each group to present its message through a stage play. I give only half an hour for preparation. This final act would not only summarize the entire workshop but also carve it indelibly in each one's memory, including mine. After all haven't liturgical dramas been part and parcel of many metacosmic religions, and all cosmic religions?

when history is re-interpreted to convey a universal truth. Take the instance of a historical novel, wherein crude facts and concrete events that are interpreted as "history" morph into a fiction capable of transmitting the lessons which that history does not and cannot expressly communicate in itself. The *history* surrounding the reign of the British Monarch Richard III, already an interpretation, has been raised to the power of *myth* in Shakespeare's dramatic version of it. His *Timon of Athens* is a timeless message about greed and the cult of the money-demon. The myth is incessantly produced and reproduced to convey the *perennial* significance of otherwise bland events recorded in the annals of human history. Transforming history into a message of redemption or reading history as a story of salvation is what we learn from the Bible.

The Exodus was a series of events woven into a history and then metamorphosed into a story that has continued to influence many emancipatory movements outside Israel down the centuries, both in the anti-slavery agitation in USA and during the Industrial Revolution in UK, not to mention its role in the emergence of liberation theologies of our own times. Similarly the appearance-stories recorded in the gospels are the only possible medium by which the early disciples both comprehended and conveyed the mystery of the resurrection of Jesus. No religion can dispense with myths understood in this particular sense. Both anthropologists and biblical theologians have recognized this particular notion of 'myth' as a name for an indispensable conveyor of truths that are to be relished intuitively.

It is equally true that mythologizing, like all good things, can also be abused. A myth can express not only a sound message of liberation but also an ideology that justifies an existent or prospective enslavement. But the abuse of a thing does not remove the possibility of its good use (*abusus non tollit usum*). So is the recourse to myths. Even the myths that legitimize an unjust social order can be exploded by a counter-myth that advocates a society of equals. The Bible resorts to this strategy very often.

Take for instance, the **Atrahasis myth** of the ancient West Asians, justifying the pyramidal structure of the imperial model of government wherein a leisure class (Priests and Rulers) live on the exploited labour of the slave class. According to this myth *gods are exempted from work and enjoy rest* while the *humans are destined by the divine will to work hard* so that the parasites among the *humans* (i.e., priests and rulers, the leisure class!) could claim a certain degree of divine character thanks to their exemption from hard labour! Such myths shocked the Jewish deportees in Babylon because their *experience* of YHWH — a God who loathed the imperial system of government which thrived on slavery and who liberated those slaving under that oppressive system— has given them another notion of both divinity and labour. Hence in the Creation Myth of the Bible the Sun and the Moon worshipped as gods are treated as mere "lamps" to *serve* humans as providers of light. And so on.

Thus it was *while in Exile in Babylon that the Israelites learnt to employ the mythical idiom of their gentile environment to refute the political ideology which was conveyed by that myth.* Their intention was to communicate their own traditional belief which was based on their experience of a God who repudiated empires where such myths as the Atrahasis myth justified the political ideology that underlies a slavery-based economy; so they **replaced this Atrahasis Myth with *another* Myth,** which turned the message of the former upside down. This new myth eventually became the first chapter of Genesis (also re-formulating another Babylonian Creation myth). It proclaimed the liberative message that *God labours* for six

141

days, whereas all that the *humans* did immediately after being created was to *rest* with God, so that they felt obliged to work with God and rest with God, their covenant partner in the labour of continuous re-creation of the universe.

When our ancestors here in Asia began a narration with the words "once upon a time there was a man or a woman", they meant that *that* man or woman is hiding in every man and woman of all times and places. Adam in the Creation Myth is one such mythical person living in all of us. Genesis III is a myth that explains, not so much the "Original Sin" as the *Origin of Sin* as experienced by all the humans of all times and places and its consequences are presented in the 'mythical' manner in the ensuing chapters. In a narration that takes relatively few words, the biblical story-tellers have described a universal truth that speculative theologians have employed volumes of paper and ink to explain under the heading *De Deo Creante et Elevante.* I do not disparage theological discourse made in writing, which is what I myself am doing here, but only wish to defend and promote the indispensable role that the oblique idiom plays in transmitting *salvific events* without diluting or distorting them into *formulated truths.*

Furthermore, it is naïve to dismiss the mythical idiom as a primitive mode of communication that suited the superstitious past and to be abandoned today in the modern scientific world. On the contrary, the mythical idiom employed lavishly in all Scriptures in the world has never gone out of date. The Jātaka stories (past lives of the Buddha) have served the Buddhists as their most accessible and effective mass-catechesis and continue to do so even today. One of our outstanding Buddhist Psychiatrists, the late Dr D.V. Harischnandra had written a best-seller on the profound psychiatric implications of those stories and used them to heal his patients through psycho-dramas in which the mentally afflicted were invited to enact the role of certain characters in such stories.[96] The Spider Man and Harry Potter, for example, are not antediluvian concoctions of a primitive generation. The film and the teledrama are but more sophisticated versions of the same thing. Even today I teach the "doctrine" of creation as a *Kerygma* on the basis of the two stories told in the first and second chapters of Genesis.

4. Jesus, the Story of God in our lives

The History of Israel has become a source of Revelation for us; it has become *our* Sinai where *we* hear the Word of God; *our* Arc that contains the Covenant.... only in so far as Israel's faith in YHWH, who acted through those historical happenings, turned *their* history into a *story of that same God* whom they believed to have been personally involved in *their* doings; in other words, **their own national history was seen as *God's story in their life.*** Here I wish to suggest that **Israel's confession of faith in YHWH who had forgivingly accepted them in every instance of infidelity turned their *national biography* into what I would call "a *theography* of Israel".** It is an invitation to Christians to read the story of this God in their own personal as well as national histories. That is why Israel's faith does not consist of a rationally organized series of credal formulations such as those we utter in our Credo every Sunday (about *Deus de Deo, Lumen de Lumine... genitum non factum...* and about *consubstantiality*) using the abstract language of ancient Greek philosophers, but a **narration of God's activities in their lives (Dt 26: 5-9;**

---

[96] I was privileged to have been invited to deliver the main address during the ceremony in which this book was officially launched at the Medical Faculty of the Ruhuna University, in Galle. In this address of mine — now available in print as a chapter in my book *Nazarathaye Jesu saha Bharataye Yesus* (Savana series no. 8, 2004) and which Dr Harischndra wished to include as the Foreword to the Sinhala version of the book that he had planned but could not realize due to his sudden death— I have highlighted the psycho-spiritual role of the *mythical mode* used in the Jātaka Stories.

143

Nehemiah Ch. 9), as the late grass-roots theologian Carlos Abesamis, s.j. of the Philippines had constantly reminded us.

In the Christian antiquity, the original meaning of the word "confession" was not a direct manifestation of one's conscience or a mere disclosure of one's sins, but a public profession of one's faith in God expressed through a grateful and praiseful narration of divine interventions in one's often unfaithful life. St Augustine's *Confessions* is a classical example of this. I myself have titled my autobiography *A Theography of My Life*. What is true of Israel as a nation is true of all individual persons, too. The Son of Man, our eschatological interpreter (Mt 25, 31-45) will give his final verdict on this story and add dimensions which we do not know ("Lord when did we....?"). The hagiographical tradition in the church restricts such stories to biographies of deceased members of the church. In many charismatic movements, there is room and even a demand for living members to make personal testimonies as part of confessing their encounter with God in their life. This was an essential part of the Kerygma, as witnessed in the case of both Paul and Peter.

The most fundamental qualification of a theologian, there fore, is to become a parable of Jesus in the way Jesus was a parable of God. The words of Jesus in John 13:34 can be accurately re-worded as follows: "As the Father has told his love-story in and through my life, so must you too tell my love-story in and through your life". God manifests God's holiness through us who remain in Her divine company (Leviticus 10:3).

5. Need for Pluralism of Symbols

Just as the absolute mystery cannot be restricted to one human mode of communication, such as say, *reason,* without ending up in contradictions, there is need for pluralism and complementariness also in the use of symbols. For when referring to the mystery of Christ (Eph 3:18), the Pauline writer employs the horizontal dimension ("length and the breadth") as well as the vertical dimension ("height and the depth"). For instance the so-called "descent Christology" which presupposes God as the One Who is "above" and humans and the cosmos as those who are "below" (depth-height dimension), helps to bring out the humility of God who comes down and the true nature of salvation as elevation (Phil. 2: 5-11) —the rich implications of which can be read in Urs von Balthasar's well known analysis of verticality. But we are equally right in indulging in an "ascent Christology" where redemption/ redeemer erupts from the cosmos itself as we sing during Advent: *aperiatur terra et germinet salvatorem, nubes pluant justum* (Let the earth split open and bud forth the Saviour; let the clouds rain down the Righteous One). It is another way of using the depth-height language. Salvation does not come down from somewhere above and beyond the cosmos, but emerges from the cosmos itself.

The Teilhardian Christology attempts a third way: it sees the "below-up" movement as a rectilinear process of evolution which climaxed in the *emergence* of the redeemer/ redemption (who/which was always there *in germine*) at a particular time in history and its gradual *convergence* into an all-embracing and all-fulfilling salvific event at an yet unrevealed moment in the future; he called this process *Christogenesis,* the gradual unfolding of the Plenitude of Revelation and Salvation. Here the depth-height idiom is replaced by the length-breath discourse. It is a happy combination of the breadth dimension of the tangential energy (of the creatures) and the length-wise pull of the radial energy (of the Creator) that accounts for the transformation of this cosmos into the New Age of the Risen Lord.

One should not, however, restrict one's language to any one of these models. For they do not contradict but complement one another. Dogmatism that can result (and has resulted) from the use of words and concepts in the rational formluatory idiom in theology should not be allowed to recur also in the words and concepts accompanying symbols. The Mystery of God in Christ defies such reductionist attempts. The Bible uses "opposites" —as fire and water, storms and stillness— to evoke the presence and activity of God. This tendency of West Asians who compiled the Bible is amply available also in the sacred writings of all Asians, in the North, South and Far East. It is *the Asian* way of communicating the mystery of salvation. In the West too this mode of transmitting truth is used in its highly developed aesthetic tradition outside the stream of scholastic theology. Thomas Aquinas the theologian was also a poet, in whose hymns, his theology becomes an aesthetically delectable prayer.

6. The Art of *Teaching* Asian Theology: The Integrated Method

There are two forms of integration we advocate. The first is in the *art of doing* theology and the second is in *art of teaching theology*. The former has already been described in detail in the forgoing chapters as the "art of theologizing in Asia". It is a method that weaves together *pastoral praxis, spiritual growth* and *pursuit of studies*. For people engaged in the apostolate often have no time for personal prayer and personal study. Those who have not learnt to integrate the three dimensions during their formation suffer from dissipation in their apostolic life. Archbishop Helder Camera's pioneering effort in this species of integrated education was unilaterally banned by the ecclesiastical powers. Bishop Leo Nanayakkara's Sevaka Sevana in Badulla (Sri Lanka) suffered the same fate. Prof. Shirley Wijeysingha, also in Sri Lanka, continues this method for the laity in his *Savana* Institute while the Asian Institute of

146

Theology (AIT) of the Oblates and Claretians is a pastoral exposure course combined with study and meant for the third year theologians. A Vatican dicastery has shown interest in this last mentioned program. While supporting the venture of AIT, I suggested that

(a) The theology professors should themselves, as formators, accompany the students in their exposure programmes and that

(b) instead of having one year of pastoral programme, we should have all the four years of theology organized in such a way as to help the formandi to *integrate* pastoral exposures, academic pursuits and spiritual growth and that such a module should be a *permanent feature* of Religious and Presbyterial formation.

Then I pushed my proposal still further: there should be a radical change in the *art of teaching theology*. I appealed to the *academic* staff to change the traditional method of **compartmentalizing theology** into various branches that run parallel without converging. This means that there should be a closer **collaboration between various professors teaching various branches of theology.** For in the current practice, a seminarian enters the presbyerial order saddled with many a 'logy' in which he has passed exams (ecclesiology, sacramentology, patrology, Christology etc etc) but without a holistic grasp of theology. The traditional way of *specializing* in various branches of theology has left the student with a number of disparate subjects *to be studied* (and tested at examinations)..... as mere *stepping stones* for the ordination; but later as a pastor he hardly uses this multifarious form of knowledge! Rather, he uses his common sense and practical wisdom based on what he understands of the scriptural reading of the day. This is the reality.

147

Hence whatever we Religious attempt to do for our men and women in theological studies —both in AIT and the future "theolgogate" we are planning to create— must change this teaching method and also set an example to the Diocesan Seminary. I am proposing just **one such change** to be introduced, something for which **we teachers are required to do some hard preparatory work.** My suggestion is that each specialist treat and teach his or her subject within the whole. Take ecclesiology as a case in point. Today a professor teaches this as a separate branch in which he is specialized. The student will study it and pass the examination well but he cannot acquire a synthesis of what he learns from each professor because each professor neither possesses nor gives a holistic view but speaks only as an ecclesiologist or a Christologist and so on. If, on the other hand the professor of ecclesiology is himself trained to **think of and teach all aspects of theology** (Christ, sacaments, patristics, eschatology, etc. etc) *from the perspective of the history and the nature of the church*, the students too will acquire a synthesis; and so on with every other "branch". Similarly, Christology is not a water-tight compartment but a *perspective* for studying various other aspects of theology: sacraments, church, God, creation, redemption and Mariology, eschatology and so on. So also a sacramentologist cannot teach liturgy with out contextualizing it within the doctrines of Trinity, God, Christ, Church, Worship, and so on and also within the framework of church history, contemporary reality, eschatology etc.

What I suggest, therefore, is this: instead treating each subject as a self-contained unit or a "specialized branch of theology", one must *learn* and *teach* each subject as **one particular *perspective* for teaching the *whole* of theology.** This is how we should understand "specialization". Thus the student is not confused and dissipated by the variety of different subjects he or she has to learn. For **in the study of**

each discipline, the whole of theology is touched. He or she realizes that theology is one and the perspectives are different, and begins to acquire a synthesis in each class, since **every professor touches all aspects of theology from within his/her own branch of specialization.** In short we need a **new way teaching theology,** and consequently **new type of theology teachers.**

What I propose here now is the method of *teaching* theology that an *academic staff* should adopt anywhere in the world, not merely in Asia. My proposal is based once more on my own experience of teaching. When I teach religious life and vows, I start with what the Scriptures reveal about these dimensions of Christian witness, and demonstrate its ecclesiological, Christological, Sacramental, eschatological, missiological and Asian-contextual implications in such a way that all these disciplines are covered in their interconnection. And that is the way I teach missiology, theology of religions, spirituality and so on. If every subject is taught in this manner, both the professors and the students would learn to avoid compartmentalization which is encouraged by the present system of theological education. For these various "disciplines" are in reality dimensions of one theological discipline. You cannot study one without integrating the others. The teachers themselves have to be holistic in their study and in their perception of various branches of theology   before they can impart an integrated vision to the students.[]

Part Three

The Written Word (Scriptures) and the Eternal Word (Christ): as Heard and Read by Asians

CHAPTER VI
Liberational Hermeneutics
Derived from Asian Sources
AN INTRODUCTORY ESSAY

A slightly revised version of an article originally published in: V. Tirimanna (ed.), *Reaping a Harvest from the Asian Soil: Towards an Asian Theology*, 2011, Bangalore (Asian Trading Company), 39-52,

1. Background Information

Although there had been a tradition of Scriptural interpretation from the inception of Christianity, the so-called 'modern' biblical hermeneutics had a rather late origin. Its beginnings are traced back to the first wave of Renaissance in the 14th century when a group of young enterprising Italian laypersons, profiting from their experience of editing and publishing the works of ancient 'pagan' Latin classics, adopted an equally critical approach to the existing versions of the Bible, discovering for the first time the need to interpret the Scripture in terms of its various *genre literaire* while abandoning at the same time the allegorical interpretation of the Patristic Era.[97] The period of the 16th / 17th centuries, the highpoint of the second wave of

---

[97] W.J. BOUSMA, "The Spirituality of Renaissance Humanism" in: J.Raitt (ed.), *Christian Spirituality: High Middle Ages and Reformation*, London, SCM Press, 1988, specially, 244-247.

152

Renaissance, marked the discovery of what was called "philology", which, as understood *then*, is said to be what we know *today* as textual criticism, literary analysis and so on.[98] These two small steps were followed by the big leap in and around the 19th century which grew into what is universally known today as 'modern' biblical exegesis.[99] No Asian theologian can afford to ignore these academic achievements of the West when interpreting the Scriptures to the people of our continent.

On the other hand, the continent of Asia, so well known as the source of the *sacred scriptures* of all existing world religions, is not yet recognized as the repository also of so many *exegetical traditions,* some of which go back to pre-Christians times! If the mere experience of editing 'pagan' Latin Classics could inaugurate a new era of hermeneutical *science* in the Christian West, could not the *art* of exegesis developed by our non-Christian ancestors do the same for Christians in Asia?

Let me leave aside the West Asian traditions of Judaism and Islam, both of which bear an affinity to Christianity, and focus on a South and South East Asian contribution, with particular reference to the Pali commentarial literature (*aṭṭhakathā*), more particularly the two monumental Buddhist treatises on hermeneutics, *Nettippakaraṇa* and *Peṭokapadesa,* which had been compiled about ten or twelve centuries before modern biblical exegesis was even thought of in Europe.[100] Very few, unfortunately, are aware of their

---

[98] J.D.TRACY, "*Ad Fontes*: The Humanist Understanding of Scripture as Nourishment of the Soul", *Ibid.,* 254-264.
[99] D.S.PACINI, "Excursus: Reading Holy Writ: The Locus of Modern Spirituality" in: L. Dupré & D.E. Saliers, *Christian Spirituality, Post-Reformation and Modern,* London, SCM Press, 1989, 195-210.
[100] I grant that the Pali exegetes were an elite class of *literati* who practised and promoted a soteriology that culminated in the family-renouncer's spirituality. Yet, unlike the corresponding *bhāṣya* literature of the Hindus, the Buddhist commentaries

153

existence, let alone acknowledge their significance or relevance for Christians. Regrettably such ignorance could also degenerate into arrogance compounded with prejudice.[101]

This essay is based not only on my doctoral thesis and thirty years of post-doctoral research in the field of Buddhist exegetical literature, some of which have already been published,[102] but also on my experience of generating an inter-textual encounter between the Hebrew-Christian Bible and the Pali Buddhist Tripiṭaka, paying due regard to their original linguistic idioms, their divergent cultural matrices, their underlying socio-political histories and their respective exegetical traditions.[103]

(specially of the Theravada School) show a remarkable 'sense of history', supplying a wealth of information about contemporary people, customs and events in the course of commenting on the *sacred text,* thus tacitly acknowledging that what the sacred texts reveal and what the *secular history* has recorded are not to be dissociated from each other.

[101] Here is an amusing example. Once I was invited by the editor of a very progressive Italian journal to provide meditations on some Sunday gospels, and I wrote them after consulting the best of West's biblical scholars and complementing their findings with insights from South Asia's own tradition of reading sacred texts. To my dismay the person commissioned to translate one of these pieces had mutilated my thought by eliminating an important observation of mine, thereby introducing an unwarranted change in my text —without having the courtesy to consult me beforehand! The amusing part of this episode is that at the end of my article he not only identified himself as the translator by name but went out of his way to append to his name his own self-description as *"biblista"* (scripture scholar)! Even if it is doubtful that any authentic scripture scholar would advertize him/herself in that *soi-disant* mode, the subtle message I received from his self-reference was very clear:- You, there, in Asia should know a thing or two from our (*my*) scientific achievements in exegesis!

[102] A series of research papers have appeared in *Buddhist Studies* (Hamamatsu, Japan), *Journal of the Post-Graduate Institute of Pali and Buddhist Studies,* and in the Festschrifts felicitating various Buddhist scholars.

[103] A. PIERIS, "Cross-Scripture Reading, Buddhist-Christian Dialogue: Search for the Right Method", P.J. Wickeri (ed.), *Scripture, Community and Mission ,Essays in Honour of D. Preman Niles,* CCA (Hong Kong),CWM (London), 2002, pp.234-255; "Two Mission Mandates Calling for Conversion: Preach the Dhamma (Vin. I. 21), Proclaim the Gospel (Mk 16:15)", *Dialogue NS,* vols. 32/33 (2005-2006), pp.1-57; "Truth and Freedom in the Tripiṭaka and the Bible: Towards an Inter-scriptural Dialogue", *Dialogue NS,* vols. 35/36 (2008-2009), pp.160-180.

I have fruitfully employed one of these studies (the one on the Buddha's and the Christ's convergent teachings on *beatitudinal spirituality of evangelical poverty demanding justice to the poor*)[104] at a seminar organized in June 2010 at our Tulana Centre under the auspices of the Peace and Justice Desk of the Methodist Church for a group of both Sinhala and Tamil participants, including socio-politically informed Sinhala Buddhist monk-activists and the clergy of Hindu, Christian and Muslim religious persuasion with a view to facilitating their engagement in a common struggle for peace and reconciliation in the post-war situation of our country. By incorporating some of Asia's traditional exegetical methods into current principles of biblical hermeneutics I succeeded in allowing both Buddhist and Christian Scriptures to come alive as a voice that spoke to them in the here-and-now of our history. It was the fruit of many years of experimentation. But what I offer here is only a glimpse into this exegetical approach.[105]

I am grateful to Dr Sam Mathews, the New Testament Professor of the Gurukul Theological Seminary in Chennai, who, after having visited our Centre to be initiated into the art of cross-scripture reading and having watched me handling the biblical texts for young Jesuits during their weekly liturgy, urged me to make this method available in writing and not to restrict it to oral transmission. This essay is the first timid step towards that bold enterprise.

2. An Ancient Principle of Exegesis

The most fundamental formula of hermeneutics runs in Sanskrit as follows: *Mumukṣave vyācikhyāsito granthaḥ.* Using the desiderative mode of the verb "to liberate" (*muc-*) and of the verb "to interpret" (*vi+ā+khyā-*), the sages

---

[104] "Cross-Scripture Reading", pp.246ff.
[105] A jejune summary of this thesis has appeared in *Spiritus* (USA), no. 11 (2010).

declare that the sacred text (*granthaḥ*) by its very nature is "longing, yearning and pining to be interpreted" (*vyācikhyāsitaḥ*) solely "for the sake of the person who is longing, yearning and pining to be liberated" (*mumukṣuḥ*). **The criterion of a good exegesis, in other words, is that it responds not only to the human heart's ardent desire for liberation (*mokṣa*) but also fulfils the sacred text's own hidden aspiration to be so interpreted as to serve that end. Like theology, exegesis, too, has to be liberational.**

Hence we should take care that our effort to equip the readers with a multiple analysis of the text in terms of its history, forms, redaction and so on (as done in the West today) should be geared to actuate the in-built *liberational potential of a given text* for the sake of readers and listeners *who yearn for freedom* from every socio-spiritual bondage; and not merely to satisfy those suffering from a 'gnostic itch' to *master* that text through a *scientific or objective knowledge* of it —a knowledge that the deconstructionists dismiss as an unachievable enterprise. This latter way of 'grasping' the texts is as fatally harmful as 'grasping' a snake in the wrong way, the Buddha would warn us, punning on the word "grasping" (*gahaṇa/grahaṇa*), which could mean "taking by the hand" as well as "understanding with the mind".[106] The implication of this warning of the Buddha is that a misapprehended text can hurt us rather than heal us! The Buddhist exegetes, therefore, place no trust in Scriptural expertise (*pariyatti*) as such unless it serves the [text's] "liberative purpose" (*nissaraṇattha*).[107] That is why I speak of the liberative *intent* rather than the liberative *content* of the sacred text.

---

[106] M.! 134-135.
[107] Cf. DA.I.21

In his famous discourse on the art of discerning the truth, the Buddha offers only one reliable criterion:- **what liberates you** from "possessiveness, rancour and self-deception" (*lobha, dosa, moha*) **is the truth,**[108] being the Buddhist counterpart of Johanine Jesus's "**Truth** [is what] **will liberate you**".[109] It is noteworthy that here the Buddha, whilst upholding the judgment of genuine practioners, i.e., the "Wise Sages" (*viññuno*) as a guiding principle in one's search for the salvific truth, quite categorically relegates "scripture-scholarship" among the *non-reliable* criteria of discernment![110] According to the exegetes, therefore, all 'scripture scholarship' (*pariyatti*) must be accompanied by *paṭipatti* (practice of what is revealed in the scriptures) climaxing in *paṭivedha* (the primordial experience of liberation).[111] The scripture scholar's exegesis, which does not lead the reader/listener, even in a small measure, to that experience (as witnessed in the praxis of the "wise", i.e., the tradition created by the liberated ones), would therefore be a profanation of the sacred text in that such an exegesis would frustrate the text's own "in-built yearning" for a liberational exegesis.

The presupposition, here, is that all scriptures of religions are a crystallization of a *collective memory of a primordial experience of liberation*, such as the Exodus and Easter in Christianity, the Buddha's attainment of *Nirvana* in Buddhism, or *advaita* experience in the Vedantic tradition, and so on. This Collective Memory, in any religion,

---

[108] A.I. 188 ff.
[109] Jn 8:32
[110] I.e., *piṭaka-sampadāna*, popularly translated as 'scriptural tradition' (< Sanskrit *sam-pra-dā*) but more probably *piṭaka-sampādana* (>Sanskrit *sam-pad*) which would mean 'accomplishment in Scripture studies' or, as Woodward has translated in the official edition, (*The Book of Gradual Sayings*, Oxford, PTS, 1989, 171-172), "proficiency in the collections" [of sacred texts].
[111] A distinction made by the exegetes on the basis of scriptures, observes NYANATILOKA (*Buddhist Dictionary*, Kandy BPS, 1997, 252).

comprises not only the written texts or the **Scriptures**, but also an unwritten **Tradition** relayed from generation to generation by means of certain characteristic life-styles of the holy ones and symbolic acts such as ritual enactments.[112] Note therefore that this manner of perceiving *the transmission of the primordial experience* avoids dualism between "**Scripture and Tradition**" that the Catholic Church was struggling to reconcile during and after Vatican II. In their exegesis, the Buddhist commentators seem to employ a *unitary perception* of the written and the unwritten versions of the Collective Memory, as indicated below.

At the heart of the Collective Memory (specially the written memory or scriptures, which is our main focus here) there lies the primordial salvific experience that originated it and therefore animates, explains, and justifies it. The Buddha had explicitly declared that his "doctrine and discipline" (*dhamma-vinaya*) is saturated with the "*taste* of liberation" (*vimutti-rasa*) just as the ocean is saturated with the taste of salt.[113] Thus the exegete, who is called to interpret the Collective Memory must not only acquire the *taste* of the primordial experience of liberation (Exodus,Nirvana, Easter), which permeates the scriptures, but also allow the text to evoke that *taste* in the reader/listener. To apply an Ignatian maxim, 'tasting things within us' (*res interne gustare*), rather than 'accumulation of knowledge' (*abundantia scientiae*)[114] is the sure guarantee of liberational hermeneutics.

3. Reason and Tradition in Liberational Hermeneutics
The laboratory method of dissecting an animal (text) and observing its parts gives one an idea of a dead animal (text).

---

[112] For a detailed exposition of this thesis illustrated with concrete historical data from both Buddhism and Christianity, see A. PIERIS, *Prophetic Humour in Buddhism and Christianity*, Colombo, Ecumenical Institute, 2005, 107-123.
[113] A. IV. 203. See also Chapter I, sections 1 & 2.
[114] Sp. Ex. No. 2

Understanding a living being requires a different approach. The sacred text that we read is not a dead letter but a **living word** conveying the power of the originating experience. **Only an exegete profoundly stirred by that primordial event can serve as the mediator in this exercise.** The Fathers of the Church, notwithstanding their allegorical mode of exegesis and their misogyny, did nevertheless exhibit an experiential knowledge of the Primordial Event that vivifies the Written Word; this is evidenced in the pastorally effective persuasiveness that characterizes patristic homiletics, something conspicuously absent in the scholastic theology of the subsequent era. They teach us that over and above the mastery of the ancient languages in which the primary sources have recorded the Collective Memory of the Originating Experience of Salvation, the exegete must also possess an intuitive grasp of and a sensitive familiarity with the *redemptive idiom* of the written memory so that he or she could facilitate the convergence of the two reciprocal aspirations of the Sacred Text and its Reader. This is the *spirituality* required of an exegete.

Even this spirituality has to be complemented by a competence to handle the "hermeneutical tool" (*hāra*) known as *yutti*, which is a sort of **a praxis-based "rational" intervention.** The literal meaning of *yutti* is 'that which is fitting or ought to be'. From my own (already published) studies on how the Pali exegetes have handled this hermeneutical tool, I have tentatively inferred that it connotes a reasoning that resonates with the original liberative experience as continued and confirmed in the traditional praxis of the Wise.[115] Thus the **unitary approach**

---

[115] See my *Studies in the Philosophy and Literature of Ābhidhammika Buddhism,* Colombo, EISD, 2004, 206-08; and my monograph, "Cardiac theory of Consciousness and Body-Mind Relationship in Post-Canonical Scholasticism", *Journal of the Post-Graduate Institute of Pali and Buddhist Studies,* University of Kelaniya, Vol 2 (2007), 204-207; "The Genesis of the Cardiac Theory of

to scripture and tradition plays a significant role in this species of hermeneutics. For these exegetes insist that an isolated scriptural text taken on its face-value (*pāli-dassanena matthena*) cannot disclose its true sense unless the pragmatic rationale (*yutti-vicāraṇa*) upheld by the "Buddhist Dispensation's uninterrupted practice" (*sāsana-yutti*) is taken into consideration; which means that the "literal meaning" (*nītattha*) has to be complemented and clarified by the "meaning [exegetically] induced" (*neyyattha*) through recourse to *yutti*, i.e., *reason mediated by the accumulated wisdom of the past.*[116]

I am intrigued by a similar method employed in the Jewish rabbinical tradition. In fact I could not have captured the liberating message of the Ecclesiastes (Qohelet) had I not read Rabbi Jonathan Sack's commentary on it. The phrase "vanity of vanities" derived from the Latin Vulgate's *vanitas* (from *vanus,* meaningless) has totally misled Christian scholars, whereas the Jewish Rabbi, who knows this work as his own ancestral heritage, brings the wisdom of the past into his rational explanation. Here the Hebrew word *hevel* (breath), misinterpreted as meaninglessness in the Christian Bible and in Christian exegesis, evokes exactly the opposite meaning! It points to the *salutary brevity of human life,* namely, to the fascinating fact that our life, in so far as it is bracketed by birth and death, is the guarantee of its enjoyability, like any symphony if it has a definite beginning and an end.[117] An endless musical composition would be horribly tedious (not to speak of a beginningless one, *per impossibile*)! The rabbinical exegesis that derives this

---

Consciousness: An Historical Reconstruction", *Buddhist Studies,* Vol. XXXIX, March 2011, pp.77-94.
[116] For relevant exegetical sources, see *Studies,* note 21 on p.186; notes 71-77 on pp. 220-21.
[117] For a neat summary of this interpretation, see Jonathan SACKS, "Recipe for Happiness: the Message of Ecclesiastes", *Vāgdevī, Journal of Religious Reflection,* 4/1 (January 2010) 22-41.

conclusion parallels the function of *yutti* in Buddhist hermeneutics.

4. The Reader/Listener as *Mumukṣuḥ*

To sum up: the key concept in exegesis is the *desire for liberation* which the sacred text is destined to fulfill in the reader through the mediation of the exegete. Cross-scripture studies on this theme has convinced me that the common denominator of the definitions of 'liberation' advocated in [the movements triggered off by] the major religions could be paraphrased as *the deliverance of the rich from the lure of riches, the poor from the burden of their enslaving **poverty** and both classes from **greed**.* I think that most social encyclicals of recent popes have been trying to communicate this noble vision, but it was left for Michael Moore to bring that message down to the level of the man and woman in the street with his powerful documentary *Capitalism: A Love Story.* The implication is not that wealth or its acquisition is evil; rather, like the meal at the Lord's Supper in Corinth, wealth too is a 'sacrament' of communion when shared, but 'a sin against the Body of the Lord' when enjoyed only by a few.[118]

The implicit conviction hidden in this definition of 'liberation' (*mokṣa, nissaraṇa, vimutti*) is that a universal deliverance from *greed* coincides with the elimination of two causally connected extremes: accumulation by one group and dispossession in the other. Only this ideal, seemingly utopian, defines a true religion and justifies its existence. Since, however, one cannot dream the impossible, all dreams are realizable through *relentless commitment* which is what "asceticism" means in any religion. Furthermore, it is always a few who struggle and drag the rest with them towards that ideal. Hence in the post-resurrectional church, the Christians

---

[118] Cf. I Cor 11:17-26

have projected this *idealism* in terms of 'alternative models' of society, where 'greed-free living' ensures the simultaneous elimination of both possessors and dispossessed.[119] How far and how long this lofty ideal was realized is a different matter. But ever since that experiment took place, the church has been challenged every now and then by such communities, specially of monastics and other vowed religious. Even those religions such as Buddhism or Jainism, which ground societal emancipation in the individual attainment of salvation have, nevertheless, projected 'contrast communities', wherein monks and nuns strive to maintain equality and fairness through a legal code (*vinaya*) geared to ensure *greedless living*. This **traditional praxis of greedless living** is an **indispensable point of reference in an exegesis** that aims at evoking "non-greed" (*mokṣa*) in the reader or listener of the Sacred Word.

Let me insist that "non-greed" is a common apophatic definition of the supreme ideal of *mokṣa* in certain religious systems. The word "greed" occurs in Buddhist literature under various guises:- *kāma* or *rāga* (lust), *lobha* (possessiveness), *taṇhā* (avarice) or *upādāna* (slavish clinging or addiction), *bahubāṇḍa-* (accumulativeness or hoarding). Hence the recommended opposite is **beatitudinal poverty**, i.e., *appicchatā* (desiring the minimum necessary) which the Buddha always qualifies as *santuṭṭhi* ('contentment', 'satisfaction' or 'beatitude'), to attain which, a generous **sharing of wealth** (*samvibhāga, dāna, cāga*) is advocated.[120] Sharing is a necessary step, albeit not the only one, towards the simultaneous liberation of the greedy and the needy.[121]

---

[119] Acts, 2:42-47; 4:32-37; 5:12-16.
[120] This thesis is documented in my "Cross-Scripture Reading", pp.246-253.
[121] Ibid.

In Christianity, too, "greed" (*pleonexia*) is _the_ Sin; for St Paul equates it with "creature-worship" (*eidololatria*).[122] Greed is contrasted with one's faith in YHWH.[123] Hence, greed (or idolatry) and the worship of the true God cannot co-exist. The cult of Wealth (Mammonolatry) leading to a plutocracy that manufactures global poverty is a highly institutionalized phenomenon today. Hence all scriptures have a liberating Word for the rich as well as for the poor. Exegesis cannot satisfy the "longing of the text" to offer salvific happiness (beatitude/contentment, *santuṭṭhi*) which is equally longed for by the reader/listener, if it fails to address these two classes of persons (the rich and the poor) individually and collectively in such a way as to advocate and initiate globally organized mechanisms for eliminating globally institutionalized Greed, specially now when its feet of clay are being exposed. Our texts must *lead* us to embrace this project of integral liberation. That is why the term *dhamma-naya*, i.e., "that which 'leads' (*naya*) one to the 'message of deliverance' (*dhamma*) contained in the text" occurs in some scripture-commentaries as a synonym for a tool of exegesis.[124] In other words, hermeneutics is the art of releasing the liberative intent of any passage contained in a "Sacred Book" (i.e., in the Memory Bank of the Primordial Liberative Event) so that the reader's/hearer's innate desire to have an *interior taste* of that event is at least partially satisfied. Perhaps I need to illustrate this with a concrete example.

5. A Sample of Liberational Exegesis

Take the episode of the rich young man, who was a *mumkṣuh,* i.e., one seeking 'eternal life' or salvation (Mt 19:16ff & parallels). In the "God Channel", I heard a preacher of the prosperity gospel proclaiming, amidst

---

[122] Col 3:5; Eph 5:5.
[123] Prov. 28;25
[124] See my *Studies*, p. 194.

boisterous amens and alleluias of approval, that only *that particular* rich man (or any other who is *singled out* by Christ) is bound to make that renunciation, not all the rich! A world-recognized Catholic authority on the *vita consecrata* has also offered his readers a dose of pseudo-consolation by warning that such statements of Christ should not be taken literally! Here 'not literally' means 'not seriously'! Still others maintain that only the 'spiritual elite', i.e., a minority of perfection-seekers practising the so-called 'evangelical counsels', are being addressed here! The implication is that not all the 'salvation-seekers' (*mumukṣavaḥ*) are required to obey this call.

The advocates of these *three currently diffused interpretations* seem to work on a different notion of liberation than ours and, consequently, fail in all the three requirements of a good exegesis:- (a) they are insensitive to the reader's thirst for greedless life, (b) unresponsive to the text's own salvific intent, and (c) inattentive to the accumulated wisdom of generations of witnesses who have lived out this Word and found happiness for themselves and for others. In their exegesis, therefore, *nītattha* (the "literal sense") suffers from not being complemented by *neyyattha* (the "meaning to be educed" exegetically on the basis of traditional praxis).

In our reading of this passage we take the opposite path which leads us to a different result. Our exegesis starts with an attempt to detect the "liberative intent of the text" in the light of the "taste of liberation" saturating the New Testament. The clue is found in the crucial question that Jesus puts to this youthful **"salvation-seeker"** (*mumukṣuḥ*) to test his authenticity, namely whether he had observed God's commandments *regarding the neighbor* (vv.18-19). For the New Testament teaches that the love of neighbor by itself

164

fulfils the requirements of the law and the prophets, i.e., guarantees one's eternal salvation.[125]

But then there is the question: "Who is my neighbour"? In the answer given in the form of a parable (Lk 10:29ff), Jesus fine-tunes the definition of "neighbor" in two ways:-

(a) **Neighbour is the *victim*** of robbery and violence whom I meet in my life's journey, whose keeper I am called to be, in that s/he demands a *price* from me —my attention, my time, my purse and the interruption of my pre-arranged program, which are all apiece with the *mokṣa* I seek (Lk 10: 33-35);

(b) **Neighbour is the *Samaritan*** who, in paying that price, became a *"neighbor to"* the victim (Lk 10:36).[126] Here, Jesus identifies the love of neighbor with our *being a neighbor to the victim of injustice*. This is an echo of the Samaratan attitude to the Jews in 2 Chron. 28:8-15

No wonder that when interviewing the young man, Jesus conspicuously avoids mentioning the three commandments relating to the exclusive worship of God! He focuses *only* on those concerning the neighbor (vv18-19) which is the ultimate proof of our love and worship of God —which coincides with 'greedless life'![127] Greed or idolatry, which prevents us from worshiping God, prevent us equally from

---

[125] Mt 7:12; Rom 13:8-10;Gal 5:14;Ja 2:8
[126] See Michael Fagenblat, "The Concept of Neighbour in Jewish and Christian Ethics" in :A-J Levine & M.Z. Brettler (Eds), *The Jewish Annotated New Testament*, Oxford University Press Inc, USA, 2011, pp. 540-543.
[127] As demonstrated scripturally in A. PIERIS, *Mysticism of Service*, Kelaniya, 2000, 73-107 as well as in *Give Vatican II a Chance*, Kelaniya, 2010, 173-177.

being a neighbor to a needy person! Since God who is our salvation is love, God is "known" (i.e., "experienced") through neighbourly love, John tells us.[128]   Hence the question Jesus poses to the young salvation-seeker is *literally* "Have you loved your neighbour?" or "Have you been a neighbour to the needy?" The young man's answer was "Yes I have" (v.20). But Jesus is not convinced; for this young salvation-seeker has not shown neighbourly love towards his poor neighbours.   Jesus demanded that he fulfilled that condition of salvation. (v.21)! No wonder that the Lord's own maternal Father, YHWH has guaranteed that if Her commandments were observed, there would be no poor among God's people.[129]

Neighbourly love is too tough for the greedy, since they are idolators; they worship wealth; they trust in riches, which they hoard for themselves rather than share with the have-nots. The text adverts to the fact that this young man's greed made him go away 'joylessly' (v.22); for 'hoarding' is not a 'beatitude', i.e., not a source of joy,[130] whereas sharing one's possessions with the poor certainly is.[131]   The young man's alliance with Mammon was a hindrance to his reliance on God who could have helped him to do the impossible which God required of him (v.26; 23-24), but the other salvation-seekers (*mumukṣavaḥ*), who were already in Jesus' company, had complied with that impossible demand (v.27). Hence the *exclusive* **worship of the one true God** (which implies redemption from "greed which is idolatry") **coincides with the *love of neighbor, i.e., being neighbourly to the needy*,** which precisely is the taste of liberation (*vimuttirasa*) permeating the Gospel of Jesus!

---

[128] I Jn 4:8
[129] Dt 15:4-11
[130] Mt 6:26
[131] Lk 12:33

Thus the 'exegetical yearning' of this sacred passage corresponds to Jesus' offer of *mokṣa* to the *mumukṣuḥ*, namely, salvation to whoever yearns for Salvation —*mokṣa* which is God Herself who has become our neighbour through Christ seeking our neighbourliness; not Mammon or Unshared Riches which creates destitution and a destitute class among our neighbours.[]

CHAPTER VII
Liberation Christology
of Religious Pluralism
APOLOGIA PRO THEOLOGIA SUA

This is an amended, expanded and more
accurately formulated version of an article
originally written for the *Lieve Troch Felicitation
Volume* and published in Portuguese, in
Theologias com sabor de Mangostao, Nhanduti
Editora Sao Bernadino de Campo, 2009, 151-160.
The first hastily written version, with quite a few
infelicitous and inaccurate formulations appears in
J-M Vigil (ed.), *Por los muchos caminos de Dios,
V: Hacia una teologia planetaria*, Quito, 2010,
126-32.

1. Fidelity and Fairness in Inter-Faith Fellowship

A Christian 'theology of religious pluralism' has to be a
blend of two imperatives:- *fidelity* to what is 'unique' to
Christian faith, and *fairness* towards every other religion's
'distinctive otherness'. But the tragedy is that even Asian
theologians who promote this ideal are not unanimous as to
what constitutes Christian uniqueness, and often also about
what is non-negotiably proper to every other religion! It is in
the context of this basic disagreement, that I am writing this
essay, which, consequently, assumes an inevitably
apologetical character, forcing me to quote from my previous

works to reiterate my point of view here. Thus a few other view-points, which are not consonant with mine, have formed the backdrop of this brief presentation, in which I strive to clarify and confirm the "liberation Christology of religions", which I have proposed to Asian theologians over the past decade or more. [Pieris, 1999, 2000, 2006].

My discovery of the identities of various religions has been the fruit of an ongoing dialogue rather than of a mere academic speculation; for many linguistic philosophers have averred that it is in and through conversation that we discover our identity. I am not theorizing, but drawing conclusions from a praxis of an inter-religious conversation and an inter-religious collaboration in that ever-failing struggle which is worth failing as much as it is worth trying: struggle for the "the liberation of *every* human person and the *whole* human person" (*salus omnis et totius hominis*), which is the ultimate goal of every religion.

To be noted, moreover, is the chasm that yawns between the West, where non-Christians are a minority in a culturally Christian ambience, on the one hand, and Asia, where the Christians are a minority living in a culturally and politically non-Christian environment as well as grappling with the problem of poverty and injustice, on the other. Regrettably some Western academicians, who are graciously accommodative towards the non-Christian minority in their Euro-American context are not that tolerant of Asian Christians who are constrained by quite another set of circumstances to think and dialogue within an altogether different paradigm. Here I am compelled to respond to such critics, too, humbly inviting them to respect the difference not only between various religions but also in the way Christians practice dialogue with other religions in differing circumstances.

The **thread of my argument** runs as follows:-

(a) The popularly accepted categorization of theological stances in terms of *'inclusivism-exclusivism-pluralism'* is avoided here. In fact both inclusivism and exclusivism presuppose pluralism; for inclusivism and exclusivism are two ways of explaining the manyness of religions, and therefore they cannot be opposed to 'pluralism' as the third alternative! Besides the word 'exclusive', as long as it expresses what is *exclusively* characteristic of a religion, is not to be rejected from the vocabulary of dialogists, as some have mistakenly suggested. Exclusiveness could also mean uniqueness, which is not to be confused with absoluteness. These considerations have led me to abandon this whole paradigm and replace it with another:- syncretism, synthesis and symbiosis [Pieris, 2004, 87ff.]. I am not going to discuss this paradigm here because the focus in this discourse is on the need to understand religious pluralism in terms of both the 'communalities' and the 'specificities' of religions.

(b) What is *common* to all religions is what all religions regard as a *soteriological absolute* (i.e., universally necessary condition for salvation, defined under 'e' below), whereas whatever is 'unique' (or 'exclusive') to a religion is the defining and distinguishing character of the soteriology which *that particular religion* is. Hence uniqueness (or exclusiveness) is *not* synonymous with superiority but merely refers to the specificity of each religion. Hence I disagree with many Western theoriticians of inter-religious dialogue who condemn indiscriminately all so-called 'exclusivistic language' without which *specificity* or the *uniqueness* of a

170

religion cannot be clearly posited; for pluralism imposes *that* idiom on our inter-religious discourse. For instance, the Buddhists alone have discovered and advocated a non-theistic perception of the process of existence as 'co-dependent co-origination'; it is *exclusive* to Buddhism. Or take the case of biblical exclusiveness in identifying the true God in terms of liberation of slaves (Ex 20:3):- not only a God joining their struggle but also becoming one of them and victimized like one of them (Philip. 2:5-11) ! For it is the specificity or the uniqueness of each religion that accounts for pluralism of religions. However, whatever is unique to a particular religion, while being *a constitutive dimension of its own soteriology,* is also *inseparable* though distinguishable from the common thrust of religiousness (or soteriological absolute) which it shares with others.

(c) Hence what is *unique* to a religion is not an optional extra for other religions. It is exactly what each religion is called to contribute to other religionists for mutual enrichment. This mutual enrichment or the integration of the other's specificity in one's own spirituality is what I mean by "symbiosis". But only those who *practise the common spirituality* of all religions (what is called the 'soteriological absolute', here) are qualified as well as able to indulge in such symbiotic exchanges in the areas specific to each religion. Inter-religious dialogue is not an exercise in speculation. For religion is not just a philosophy (*darśana*) which we can discuss from a critical distance but is simultaneously a praxis (*pratipadā*) to which we commit our life. Hence we avoid the prevalent tendency [in the West] to drive a wedge between religion and philosophy.

(d) Two examples:- the practice of mindfulness as a path of liberation is no where developed to such sublime perfection as in Buddhism so that the Christians who live in a Buddhist ethos are summoned to appropriate it within their own *Christian* soteriology as I have demonstrated by unearthing the biblical version of mindfulness hidden in the Hebrew and Christian scriptures, granted that the latter would not be an exact equivalent but only a homologue of Buddhist mindfulness [Pieris, 2008b, 187-91; revised version, *Spiritus*, 10/2010, 38-56; updated version *Our Hidden Agenda* Ch. VIII]. Conversely, the justice dimension specific to biblico-Christian Theism (Part II) could be appropriated by Buddhists within their own non-theistic spirituality through a similar exercise of cross-scripture reading. [Pieris 2003, 246-53]. Such exchanges are one of the aims as well as one of the natural consequences of inter-religious encounters.

(e) The *beatitudinal spirituality*, or the 'happy life' which knows neither 'hoarding' nor 'anxiety', as advocated in both Luke and Matthew, is the **Christian version of the *common* soteriological absolute,** but spelt out in theistic categories in some religions and in a non-theistic idiom in others. On the other hand the *belief in God crucified in Christ who is One Body with the Oppressed* defines **Christianity's *uniqueness*.** This is the thesis we propound and defend here.

(f) This thesis of ours runs counter to the rabid fundamentalism of certain Christian sects on one extreme, and to the well-meant eirenism of some Christian dialogists on the other. The Christian fundamentalists preach the Crucified (and Risen) Jesus but omit the fact that the victims of injustice

172

(even non-Christians who are oppressed!) form one body with Christ on the Cross. On the other hand, some dialogists, too, fear to emphasize the *social conflict* which constitutes the Cross of Christ (scandal to the Jews and folly to the Gentiles) and therefore they compromise Christianity's uniqueness either by adopting the allegedly non-confrontational idiom of certain Indic religions such as Buddhism or by claiming for such religions a spurious equivalent of Christianity's uniqueness (examples given below). Both groups, according to our perception, fight shy or fall short of proclaiming the identity mark of Christianity: the centrality of the Cross, which is where Christ, who is one body with the victims of oppression, announces *his* as well as *their* paschal victory, and which offers also the victimizers the opportunity for conversion and salvation.

Regrettably, a Catholic version of the fundamentalist approach mentioned above (see 'f') mars the twelve documents issued on Asian theologies and Asian theologians by the Congregation for Doctrine of Faith (CDF).[132] Understandably, the CDF's criterion of orthodoxy is the traditional Christology traced back to Chalcedon. It is on the basis of *that* Christology (as developed down the centuries) that the CDF judges the Asians to be "relativists" who allegedly deny the 'uniqueness of Christ'! In *our* vocabulary, we speak of the 'uniqueness of Jesus' as his Christhood, so that the phrase 'uniqueness of Christ' sounds tautological in *our* ears (see pp.28-33 above!). Besides, our critics within the CDF do not seem to concede that the Chalcedonian Christology has utterly failed to define, leave alone defend, the uniqueness of Jesus for Asians, and that for two reasons:-

---

[132] These documents are listed in John Allen Jr, "Perils of Pluralism", *National Catholic Reporter,* September 15, 2000, 222.

173

(i) because the idea of incarnation around which it revolves seems, from an Asian point of view, to have reduced God-Man Jesus to a mere cosmic power (*deva*), one among many in the Asian pantheon, appearing "from time to time" (*yuge yuge*) in the world as *avatars*; and

(ii) because the message that God was crucified in Christ who forms one body with the oppressed — which is what defines Christianity's uniqueness— is conspicuously absent in that Chalcedonian formula [Pieris, 2000, 194-96; 209-211]. For the scandal of the cross did not begin with an 'incarnation understood as *God becoming human*' (for God is compatible with humanity which is God's own creation, something God Herself found to be good); the scandal begins with an incarnation in which *God becomes a social outcast* or one of Rome's slaves, as indicated in the manner of his death (Philip 5:2-11) —slavery being a sinful creation of humans, totally incompatible with divine love.

Our contention, therefore, is *not* that traditional Christology is wrong in what it says, *but* that it is soteriologically deficient and incapable of depicting Jesus' uniqueness before the Asians. By incarnation we do not simply mean the Logos *assumed human nature* in the abstract; but that "The Word *became flesh* (*sarx egeneto*)", i.e., he became one of us in all our human vulnerabilities which make him so much an *Immanuel,* a unique God never heard of generally in Asian mythologies. Some Western theologians who are familiar with the Asian reality have empathized with our view and have endorsed the "Covenant Christology", which we have proposed as a possible alternative to the traditional one [Neuner 213-14; also Waldenfelds, 220-21].

The Covenant Christology, which we propose, is as simple and profound as the one that Jesus implied when he *summed up* the whole of revelation and salvation in the two inseparable love commands: Love your God and Love your Neighbour. Hence even Christ Jesus, who *sums up* (or "recapitulates" as Paul puts it) in Himself the whole of revelation and salvation, ought to be the embodiment of these two love commands, which, like Him, are the sum and substance of revelation and salvation! This is the *foundation* of a Christology, which unlike the Chalcedonian one, holds together the common basis of all religions as well as the distinctive character of Christian soteriology, simultaneously leaving ample room for other religions to offer their unique contribution to Christians.

This is the foundational thesis, which we spell out below in Sections 2 and 3 of this chapter, and which can be outlined as follows:-.

Option for God   (practice of evangelical poverty, i.e., no *other* god)

     The first love-command is epitomized in the *non-idolatrous* spirituality of interior freedom consisting of greedlessness. It is the **spirituality common to all religions,** even non-theistic ones, but formulated in a *theistic* idiom by Jesus in the Sermon on the Mount in Matthew and in the Address on the Plain in Luke as *beatitudinal* life. It was Jesus' understanding of the first commandment of the Decalogue: "Yahweh alone, no other gods," (Ex,20:2-3), i.e., 'yes' to God (evangelical obedience) and 'no' to Mammon (evangelical poverty).

Option for the Poor (solidarity with the victims of social poverty)

The second love-command, not at all absent in other religions, takes on a radically new format unique to biblical Christianity on two counts taken together:-

(I)   because Jesus (in the parable of the good Samaritan) fine-tunes the concept of one's "neighbor" not only as **(a)** the *victim* of violence, whom one meets in one's life's journey, dictating a total change of one's pre-arranged programme and spelling out Eternal Life (salvation) in terms of the service one renders to him or her, but also as **(b)** the one who is a *neighbour to* the oppressed one in rendering that service (cf. Chapter VI, Section 5);

(II)   because Jesus himself has opted to become *that* neighbour by being himself a victim of violence —so that God's alliance and identification with the oppressed (who, consequently, are one Body with Christ) defines our mission as a death-defying undertaking to *be a neighbor to* such victim-neighbours.

The understanding of *Christ and his mission within the framework of the two love commands,* is the source and basis of the Liberation Christology of Religious Pluralism, which I have proposed in the past and which I am now going to reiterate in simpler terms.

2.The *Common Spirituality* that Underlies Religious Pluralism

My colleague and friend Jude Lal Fernando, enthused by a thesis presented by Regina Schwartz, the professor of English Literature at North Western University, Evanston, claims that the constitutive dimension of biblical revelation, almost a canon within a canon, is not God's option for, or covenant with, the poor (as I have always maintained) but the *pluralism and plenitude* offered by the whole of Creation to humankind, and the gift of land which is never to   be partitioned and possessed as private property but to be enjoyed by all [Fernando, 369-70].

Before I entice the two authors into a dialogue with me, I wish to complete their partial picture by adding an important dimension that they have missed out:- the "pleasure park", which this cosmos was destined to be (Gen.2:10), with its vegetation providing bodily nourishment as well as aesthetic gratification (2:9). Hence going beyond what Schwartz and Fernando claim, I maintain that all *pain and suffering* caused by injustice and inequalities results from violating and vitiating this **cosmic order** of *plenitude, pluralism* and *pleasure*! Underline *cosmic order.*

But this "cosmic" view, with due respect to these two writers, is *not unique* to biblical revelation, *nor,* therefore, the canon within the canon in biblical revelation; it is the *common ideal* of most major religions and the essence of *all* primal religions. It is the universal and original revelation, conserved up to this day in tribal and clannic cultures that still survive in many pockets of Asia, Africa and the Americas; it is the first fruits gained by the evolutionary process when the hominized beast was humanized into a *homo religiosus.* Hence it seems to be   a **pre-biblical and extra-biblical vision,** that is to say, something that the Hebrew Tradition assimilated but was careful to trace back to Yahweh, enthroned as the Supreme and transcendent Author and Authority over Nature (Gen1:1-

-2:25) and experienced and recognized as God of justice and freedom, a faithful partner in an anti-slavery campaign (Ex.20:1-3). Thus in the biblical version of this primordial *cosmic* spirituality, God holds us "co-responsible" (Gen.1:26) for fostering this healthy **cosmic order of a shared abundance,** and treats us as 'co-creators', calling us to 'work over' or 'serve' *('ābad)* the cosmic reality for human benefit (Gen. 2: 5;15). God, therefore, is our covenant partner in the struggle against plutocracy that manufactures *scarcity and suffering* in a world destined by God to be a paradise of *plenitude and pleasure.*

From Shirley Lal Wijesinghe, an Asian biblical scholar, who has gone beyond *mere* literary criticism of texts and has followed J-L Ska's lead in recognizing the strong symbolism of the ancient West Asian culture as well as its socio-political history, I have come to learn (*contra* Schwartz) that the chain of violence initiated by Cain reflects a "crisis of brotherhood" resulting from an exploitation of Nature in a *'civilization'* which was based on innate compulsive tendencies ("serpent"; "dust") rather than on the exercise of free-will ("tree of the knowledge of good and evil"), and which would end up building a megapolis (symbolized in Enoch); whereas Abel, by contrast, represents freedom from compulsions within a cosmic spirituality that ensures *plenty and pleasure* [Cf. Wijesingha, 47-51]. This is the opposite of what Schwartz had read *into* these texts.

It would seem that, here, the Bible criticizes the concept of *civilization* (symbolized by Megapolis and Babel), which even today is traced back to the rise of cities and the invention of writing. Cosmic religiosity according to this misconception is uncivilized! The one-time popular and yet ironic reference to the 'noble savage' was a reluctant concession to the humaneness, virtue and integrity of the **oral and rural** *"culture"* of primal societies 'admired, by those of

178

a **literary** and **urban** *"civilization"*. Writing restricts thinking to unilinear logical process to the detriment of the creative third eye that Nature has bestowed on humans and to the oblique idiom in communication. Cities remove humans from their cosmic habitats and turn them into Nature-hostile animals who would soon see their civilization raised to the *earth* by the same earth's natural powers such as floods, fires and quakes. The gap between Creation and Humans constitutes a negation of cosmic spirituality.

Unfortunately, it is only in the Bible that some of today's Creation-Theologians meet this primal or cosmic spirituality for the first time! No wonder, they conclude rather naively that it is unique to the Bible! The probable reason for drawing this false conclusion seems to be that the *non-biblical* (i.e., Hellenistic, moralistic and speculative) Christianity which Europe developed during the centuries after its conversion had eliminated the European version of this 'primal religiosity' as mere nature-worship or superstition. Even the remnants of primal religions were eliminated during the time of the Reformation and the Counter-reformation as vestiges of paganism. The wheat had been removed with the weeds! Thus the much needed and much aired discourse of some creation theologians on eco-spirituality hides a nostalgia for a paradise of plenty and pleasure which their European ancestors had eliminated as non-Christian or pagan in the name of an impoverished or de-biblicized Christianity!

Hence it is quite understandable that the species of Christianity that the missionaries brought to Asia from Europe had adopted the same negative posture towards Asia's own primal religions, as the Asian Bishops have observed and even criticized (*FABC Papers*, no 81, p.25). Furthermore, science and technology, which had developed in the West along the Cartesian vision of "Man exploiting

179

Nature", has now erased from history the memory of the "human-cosmic alliance" of ancient times. The result is a *technocracy*, i.e., technology allied to a *"secular* (or non-sacred) *this-worldliness"*, which is now swallowing up the *"sacred this-worldliness"* of Asia's 'cosmic religions'. The signs of the times summon the advocates of both biblical and non-biblical versions of this *cosmic spirituality* to join forces to resist *such* technocracy (and *such* Christianity!) from continuing to produce scarcity where there is plenty [Pieris 2005, 171-77].

This cosmic religiosity, which *reveres this world as sacred,* should, therefore, serve as the *common foundation* on which all religions must meet and celebrate religious pluralism as a gift to humanity, appreciating and encouraging one another's unrepeatable identities. Most anti-religious and anti-pluralist fundamentalists responsible for today's inter-religious conflicts do not seem to practise this common spirituality! It is they who invoke various 'isms' (including monotheism) to justify their monocratic programs, and even pogroms. In any history, an idolatry invoking divine will to justify *violence* is internally critiqued thanks to the soteriological absolute that each religion spells out in its own categories. In the history of Israel recorded in the Bible, this critical religious stance is an *option for God YHWH,* whose vehement opposition to accumulated Capital or undistributed wealth (Mammon) which creates poverty, has found concrete expression in *YHWH's defence pact with the victims of Mammonolatry.* This is the canon within the canon. Hence the root of all evil, including violence, is certainly not to be traced back to the 'isms' (including monotheism) invoked by religious bigots to justify their fanaticism (even within the Bible), but to their *idolatry,* which St Paul identifies with *greed* (Col 3:5; Eph. 5:5).

In Jesus' beatitudes, an Asian hears the echoes of a cosmic spirituality common to all religions:- "the happy life" (beatitude) of *sharing Nature's abundance* like the birds in the air and the lilies in the field *without hoarding* and *without anxiety* (Mt 6: 19-34; Lk 12:22-34). For Jesus, the opposite of faith is 'anxiety' leading to 'hoarding' (the source of today's scarcity and suffering) and perhaps not so much 'doubt' or 'reason' as in the non-cosmic theologies of the Western Patriarchate. In the preaching of Jesus, therefore, a universally accepted spirituality is articulated in the idiom of biblical theism, namely, as an exercise of "faith" (*'ĕmûnāh*), meaning *anxiety-free reliance*) in a Father-Mother God who is "faithful", (*'ĕmet*, or absolutely reliable). Hence one's trust in such a trustworthy God excludes any reliance on other 'gods' (Ex. 20:2-3), who are symbolized by Mammon, which is 'Unshared Wealth' as well as 'absolutization of what is relative', such as colour and caste, religion and race, language and land.

Since such idolatry is 'greed' (Col.3:5;Eph 5:5), we acknowledge that those Asian religionists who are not God-believers in the biblical sense, are nevertheless *anti-idolatrous Mammon-repudiators* in that they practise and promote *greedless* living, which is the *sine qua non* for shared abundance. Thus the "God-Mammon conflict" is the *specifically* Christian formulation of a *common* religious heritage. Hence our faith in the enfleshed Word, crucified and risen must culminate in a Christological confession: "Jesus is the irreconcilable contradiction between God and Mammon". That is the characteristically Christian formulation of the *common spirituality of all religions*. It is a Christological paraphrase of the first commandment of the Decalogue.

3.Christianity's *Uniqueness* and its Specific Contribution to Inter-religious Exchange

Whenever and wherever the Money-Demon's clients threaten to replace *plenitude, pluralism and pleasure*, respectively, with *penury, plutocracy and pain* through exploitation and hoarding, YHWH cannot and does not remain neutral as She is *bound by a covenant* to identify Herself with the victims of that sinful option, which is to say, *the Covenant with the runaway-slaves of Egypt ratified on Sinai and renewed by Christ on Calvary*. It is not surprising, therefore, that the **justice** for which the poor cry to heaven in at least 40 of the psalms, as a Scripture Scholar has explained, is an appeal to **God's** (covenantal) **love and fidelity towards the poor,** in stark contrast with **God's wrath towards their oppressors,** *orgē tou Theou* [Lyonnet, 63], i.e., **the anger of the victims appropriated by Yahweh, their defense-ally.** Hence our *unique* contribution to inter-faith dialogue is to confess (our second article of faith) that **Jesus is God's defense-pact with the poor** —not by mere words but by actively joining God's own defense of the poor. Such activity could never be a threat to other religions, because its main thrust is *not* **a conversion of other religionists to Christianity** *but* **the conversion of the chaos of induced scarcity into the order of shared abundance through greedless living.** All religionists can join this struggle without compromising their faiths.

I would have ceased being a Christian theist if YHWH of the Bible was incapable of anger that threatens hell-fire on oppressors in the name of their voiceless victims—not in order to destroy them for ever (that would be hatred), but to elicit their conversion and thus bring relief to the outcasts. For *prophetic anger is an expression of redemptive love*. The parable of the Last Judgment (Mat 25) is Good News to the poor, because the *threat* of eternal damnation jolts the non-poor from their complacency before the plight of their needy brothers and sisters. God of the Hebrew and Christian

Scriptures does not address the powerful and the powerless in the same language; nor should we!

The Hitlers, Pinochets, and Bushes had their way because their pastors failed and even feared to announce Jesus Christ as God's Defense Pact with the oppressed! For Christian fundamentalists (including those in the evangelistic fringe of the main-line churches) dilute the notion of "God's Wrath" by *spiritualizing* or de-socializing it; they dissociate it from the Covenantal justice of God so that the violence against the poor disappears from the concerns of *their* God and from *their* theology of "atonement" or "appeasement of God's wrath" [Pieris, 2008a, 13-16].

What these fundamentalists have done through a misguided evangelism, we *dialogists* could do through genuine irenism. Paul Knitter, in the process of trying sincerely to accommodate Thich Nhat Han's and Rita Gross's Buddhist critique of Liberation Theology, expresses some uneasiness about the 'aggressive' expressions such as Jon Sobrino's phrase "anti-Kingdom" or my own reference to Jesus as the "defense pact" between God and the poor [Knitter, 199-200]. His argument seems to be that an Asian theology of liberation based on God's Covenant with the poor, invoking the notion of divine anger against the victimizers, smacks of the confrontational idiom of the Bible, which allegedly sounds offensive to non-Christian Asians who employ the language of non-violence.

This uneasiness can perhaps be traced back to three unexamined assumptions. The first is the false equation of *anger* with *hatred*. The forgiving love in Christianity encompasses prophetic anger but excludes rancour. The Apostle's advice to "become angry without sinning" (Eph 4:6) insinuates that there is a legitimate place for a non-hateful anger in the life of a Christian and in the life of God. I

183

would gently remind Thich Nhat Han, Rita Gross and other Buddhist critics, as well as Western Christian dialogists who concur with them, that even the Buddhist Scriptures allude to monk-saints "burning" with holy indignation against their errant colleagues (Vinaya III, 137,138), indicating that Buddhism too differentiates between anger and hate.

The second assumption emanates from a dubious method of inter-religious accommodation —a methodological error, which I have already illustrated from the writings of Thic Nhat Hahn himself [Pieris 2003, 241]. To compromise the distinctive character of Christianity in the name of inter-religious harmony is to eliminate one partner of dialogue altogether! And, here, we are dealing with a non-negotiable element in the Biblical Christianity, just as non-theism is a non-negotiable factor in Thervada Buddhism. Each religion's uniqueness, which is not to be equated with absoluteness or superiority, constitutes the foundation of religious pluralism, and therefore the *raison d'etre* of inter-religious dialogue. Even irreconcilable differences between religions offer a message to be shared amongst all religionists as explained and illustrated above (Introduction, c & d).

The third source of misapprehension is the failure to understand the **nature of God's defense strategy** illustrated in the incarnate, crucified and risen Word in whom God and the victims of injustice constitute one sole covenanted, and therefore salvific, Reality. For in Jesus we meet both partners of the covenant: God and the oppressed. This union between the Divine Word (*dābār*) and the oppressed of the world, forming one covenantal/salvific reality, that is to say, *One Body* or ***One Corporate Person***, demonstrates **two kinds of resistance to violence**:-

On the one hand Jesus exercises God's wrath against the *wicked* who exploit the *weak,* i.e., the

184

weak whom he befriends as the inheritors of God's Reign; on the other hand, the same Jesus offers forgiveness rather than divine wrath to *his own* persecutors.

To put it in another way:- in the *life and work* of Jesus we see God's wrath being unleashed on the violators of the vulnerable, but in the *passion and death* of Jesus, we see God identifying Herself with the vulnerable so indistinguishably as to become the Violated One, who dares to defy His violators by braving the atrocities of torture unto death, *thus* engraving in the annals of human history that it is *deicide* to rob the poor of their life! Hence God's option for the oppressed symbolized in the Crucified One is not an option for violence; rather it is a divine protest against all violence. This conclusion should clear the prevalent prejudice against Asian or any other Christology of Liberation.

This kind of God and this kind of divine involvement with the oppressed as revealed in Jesus is unique to Christianity. My admired friend and colleague Michael Amalados' claim that Hinduism advocates such a God does not seem to have any foundation in Hindu scriptures as I have already argued [Pieris 1999, 83-89]. No theologian, who is at the same time a qualified and recognized Indologist, has so far produced a single instance of such a belief from any Indic religious tradition.[133] By saying this, I do not claim that Christianity is

---

[133] When asked to comment on my response to him, Amalados has not adduced a counter argument but merely dismissed my challenge saying that I am playing with the word 'poor' [Ann Alden, 123] when in reality the term 'poor' is not my invention but a blanket term recurrently used in the Hebrew and Christian *Scriptures* (as the writings of the Indian Scripture scholar George Soares-Prabhu have amply demonstrated); besides, it is an expression which I have taken pains to

185

superior to these religions, but merely indicate where and how it differs from them.

To sum up: A twofold Christopraxis conceals a Christology of Religious Pluralism. Our fidelity to our own Christian identity requires, in the first place that we proclaim Christ as the One who demands conversion from mammon-worship (Mt 6:19-24) rather than conversion from other religions (Mt 23:15), thus *confirming the common spirituality* of all religions within our own distinctively specific faith; this is the first dimension of Christology that our *common* vocation to evangelical poverty entails. Secondly, in keeping with our *Christian uniqueness*, we must confess from that common platform, both by word and deed, in liturgy and life that Christ Crucified and Risen is God's defence pact with the oppressed, so that our action-filled confession of this distinctive feature of our faith would drive us to a relentless struggle for justice and peace, as the mission of *the seed that must die to bring forth life*, rather than a *weed that kills the religious identity of others in the name of evangelization*. The other religionists can join such a struggle for justice and peace without compromising *their* faith, as is amply attested in many multi-religious "Basic Human Communities" in Asia today.[]

---

spell out in terms of *all the concrete categories of the poor* mentioned in the Scriptures, with such insistence and clarity in so many of my writings that 'playing with the word' (which Alden too repeats without substantiating the statement) is, to say the least, *a lame response to my challenge*. I am still waiting patiently for an *honest* attempt at procuring a counter-demonstration !

BIBLIOGRAPHY (For CHAPTER VII)

ALDEN, Ann, *Religion and Dialogue in Late Modernity*, Lund, Sociologiska Institutionen, 2004.
ASIAN BISHOPS, "FABC (Federation of Asian Bishops' Conferences) *Papers*, Hong Kong, No. 81 (undated).

FERNANDO, Jude Lal, "God of Plenitude and Meditation on Conscience: Subverting Religious Narratives for Peaceful Coexistence", in: J. O'Grady and P.Scherie (eds), *Ecumenics from the Rim: Explorations in Honour of John D'Arcy May*, Muenster, LIT Verlag, 2007, 369-377.

KNITTER, Paul, "Is God's Covenant with Victims a Covenant against Oppressors? Aloysius Pieris and the Uniqueness of Christ" in: R. Crusz, M. Fernando & A. Tillekeratna, Colombo, *Encounters with the Word: Essays to Honour Aloysius Pieris*, Colombo, Ecumenical Institute for Study and Dialogue, Colombo, 2004, 195-208.

LYONNET, Stanislaus, *Il Nuovo Testamento alla luce dell'Antico* (Lectures given in 1968), Brescia, Paedeia,1971, reprint 1977.

NEUNER, Josef, "Mission Theology after Vatican II".*Vidyajyoti Journal of Reflection*, 58 (April 1994), 201-214.

PIERIS, Aloysius [1999], *God's Reign for God's Poor: A Return to the Jesus Formula*, Kelaniya, Tulana Research Centre, 1999.
_____ [2000], "Christ beyond Dogma. "Christ Beyond Dogma: Doing Christology in the Context of the Religions and the Poor", *Louvain Studies*, 25, 2000, 187-231.
_____ [2003], "Cross-Scripture Reading in Buddhist Christian Dialogue: A Search for the Right Method", in: WICKERI, J. Ed., *Scripture, Community and Mission. Essays in Honour of D. Preman Niles*, London, CWM / Hong Kong, CCA, 2002 second printing, 2003, 234-255

_____[2004] *Prophetic Humour in Buddhism and Christianity*, Ecumenical Institute, Colombo.

_____ [2005], "Asian Reality and the Christian Option: A Plea for a Paradigm Shift in Christian Education in Asia", in: *Dialogue, NS,* Colombo, Ecumenical Institue for Study and Dialogue, Vol. xxxii-xxxiii, 2005-6,

_____ [2006], "Lo Spirito Santo in Asia", in: M. Amalados and R. Gibellini (eds), *Teologia in Asia,* Brescia, Editrice Queriniana, 2006, 383-410.

_____ [2008a], "What *On Earth* is God Doing to Us? Towards recovery of Authentic Christina Theism, *Gleanings,* Colombo, Ecumenical Institute for Study and Dialogue , XXVII/1 & 2 (January-June 2008), 3-16.

_____ [2008 b] "Spirituality of Mindfulness: The Biblical and Buddhist Versions", in: P.Gnanaprakasam and E.Schessler Fiorenza (Eds), *Negotiating Borders, Theological Reflections in the Global Era Essays in Honour of Prof. Felix Wilfred,* Delhi, ISPCK, 2008, 185-198. Revised version in *Spiritus* (USA), 10 (2010), 38-51)

WALDENFELS, Hans, "Christ Beyond Dogma: Some Remarks about Aloysius Pieris' Renewal of Christology", in: R. Crusz, M.Fernando & A,Tillekaratna (Eds), *Encounters with the Word: Essays to Honour Aloysius Pieris,* Colombo, Ecumenical Institute for Study and Dialogue, 2004, 209-224.

WIJEYSINGHA, Shirley Lal, "Cain and Abel: Brotherhood in Crisis ", in : *Vagdevi, Journal of Religious Reflection,* I/2 (July 2007), 45-52.

Part Four

A Summary of the Whole Book

CHAPTER VIII
A Theology of Religion
Dictated by the Poor
TOWARDS A RECOVERY OF
OUR CHRISTIAN IDENTITY IN ASIA

A revised version of a paper which was originally
read (in absentia) at the Felicitation of Gustavo
Gutierrez and Virgilio Elizondo, Notre Dame
University, Indiana in 2002 and became a chapter in:
Daniel G. Groody (ed.), *Option for the Poor in
Christian Theology*,(University of Notre Dame,
Indiana, 2007, pp. 271-289).

(I) Christianity's Identity Crisis

1. Early Beginnings
It is common knowledge that the transition from the
evangelical simplicity of the nascent church to the pyramidal
structure of Romanized Christianity began not long after the
birth of the Christian community. The first signs of a *loss of
Christian identity* can be detected already in the New
Testament period. The pastoral letters indicate that the
previous generation's ideal of equality in class, race, and
gender (Gal. 3:28), a distinguishing mark of a Jesus
community, had faded away into the Greek and Roman social
mores of women and slaves living in submission to advisedly

190

benign masters and husbands.[134] "For the householder in the church of the pastorals is rewarded for being male, prosperous, respectable, and a competent household manager"[135] Therefore, "The equality and mutuality of his followers which Jesus taught and encouraged and which was amply evidenced in the gospel narratives was by this time a dim memory and a discarded reality."[136]

There is a reason for this decline. Despite Paul's remark that most of the early converts did not come from the wise, powerful, and noble strata of society (1 Cor. 1:26), by which he might *not* have meant that only menial slaves constituted the communities he speaks of,[137] there is evidence of an unhealthy influence of the social elite (1 Cor. 11:20 – 22, 33 – 34) or perhaps even of aristocrats.[138] As the number of converts increased, first among the Jews and then among the Gentiles, the inevitable *reliance on the rich*, who not only financed the first missions but also allowed the use of their spatial mansions for liturgical gatherings, must have had its impact on the selection and quality of church leaders and consequently also on the social relationships forged among Christians. Undoubtedly, the rich were bound by the Gospel to share their resources with the community to relieve the poor and, by extension, to support the missions that brought good news to the poor; however, they would not be sharing a gift but only buying position and power within the believing community if thereby a class division were to set in. Did the advice given in 1Timothy 6:17 presuppose such a situation? That is why even in the case of the women-leaders in the

---

[134]   E.J. Cwiekowski, *The Beginnings of the Church* (New York: Paulist Press, 1988), pp. 140-42
[135]   H. Hendrickx, *The Household of God* (Quezon City: Claretian Publications, 1992), p. 119
[136]   Ibid, p. 120
[137]   Cwiekowski, *Beginnings of the Church*, pp. 119-20
[138]   R.E. Brown, *An Introduction to the New Testament* (New York: Doubleday, 1997), p. 68

191

nascent church, I ask myself whether their leadership role was recognized on the basis of *gender*-equality —which would be commendable— or on the basis of their wealthy *class*-status.

This is a *problem endemic to the church then and now*. It seems to have started with the apostles, who certainly gave up all things to follow the Gospel but continued to hanker after power and position already during the earthly life of Jesus (Matt. 9:33-35). The Gospels make it clear that here we are dealing with a temptation that even Jesus had to overcome (Matt. 4:1-11). The thirst for power that the Servant-Messiah renounced became the temptation of the nascent church. The picture that Matthew draws of his church is not flattering. The parable of the wicked tenants (Matt.21:43) warns that authority will be transferred from a sterile leadership to one that bears fruit; the Parable Discourse (Matt. 13) speaks of a mixture of the good and the bad among the disciples, and the Community Discourse (Matt. 18), addressed to the leaders of the community, speaks of "little ones," precious to the Father in heaven, who need to be protected from the scandals of the bigger people, such as perhaps the high-ranking money-handling official who was unmerciful toward an erring brother of a lower rank.[139] The leadership, which was called upon to serve as the *stable rock* on which the community was to rest (Matt. 16:18) became a *stumbling block* (scandal) when it opted for a Christ without a cross (Matt. 16:23), that is, for a power-wielding messianism.[140]

---

[139] H. Hendrickx, "Image of the Church in the New Testament," *Japanese Missionary Bulletin* 8 (1978): pp. 413-14

[140] H. Hendrickx, "Matthew and the Church, Then and Now," *Japanese Missionary Bulletin* 8 (1978): pp. 535-36

2. The Rich and the Church

How the guiding principle of *equality*, once an identifying feature of the church, disappeared had everything to do with the way the church handled the rich and their riches —or was it also the way the rich and their riches handled the church? Apart from the aforementioned changes that took place in the late New Testament period of the pastorals, there was another taking place in the post-New Testament era, specially after the Roman persecutions, when Christianity began to gain an elevated social standing in an increasingly decadent empire, thanks especially to mixed marriages between the gentile elite and Christian women.[141] Hence Christianity's respectability, so gained, was merely recognized, not created, by the Imperial Edict of Constantine. In these circumstances, a Christianized empire could not avoid being, in course of time, a social embodiment of an imperialized Christianity which has continued to our own times through the middles ages when a highly secularized or *worldly church* was dominating a culturally *religious World* (in Europe).[142] In fact, yesterday's colonization and today's globalization, in which this same species of Christianity serves rather than challenges the empire of Mammon, is a monumental witness to a loss of Christian identity.

If this is the information derived from the Scriptures and from the history of the church, our response to a similar identity crisis that the church of our own time is passing through will not be a naïve regression to the Church's *beata infantia* (blessed infancy) with Spirit possessions and mass conversions, as some zealous Christian sects maintain on the basis of Acts 2, but something less triumphalistic and more

---

[141] See Ann Yarbrough, "Christianization in the Fourth Century: The Example of Roman Women," *Church History* 45 (June 1976): pp. 149ff
[142] "While the [Western] world became, at least culturally , universally Christian, the church was becoming profoundly secular" (S. Schneiders, "The Word in the World ", *Pacifica*, 23/3, October 2010, p.249).

challenging as discussed in **Section 3** below, namely, a prayerful reflection on the *nascent church's struggles and failures to remain faithful to the spirit of Evangelical poverty* as well as a sincere effort at learning *how to regulate the role of the rich and their riches in the day-to-day life of a Jesus-community*, a community whose essence is the discipleship of equals.

Furthermore, no community can claim to be Christian unless it is animated by the Spirit of Christ dwelling in the little ones. These little ones are not only those who become one family with him by their obedience to the Word (Matt. 12:49) but also the victims of human neglect, who by that very fact become Christ's own presence in the world demanding our attention (Matt. 25:36ff). These two categories of the poor (mentioned also in Matthew's and Luke's beatitudes respectively) are citizens of God's reign and therefore members of Christ's body, the dwelling place of the Spirit. The Charismatic claims to be possessed by the Spirit, as well as their appeal to mass manifestations of mystical outpourings as divine authentication of such claims, must be tested by the infallible criterion given by the end-time judge whose presence is revealed in the victims of nations (Matt. 25:36ff). Solidarity with the poor is fidelity to the Spirit.

3. Two Anti-Imperial Strategies of the Nascent church

Our first task, as mentioned above, is to learn from the earliest Christian experiment the art of resisting the reign of Mammon. Even if that experiment seemed to have failed, it was an experiment worth failing; therefore it is an experiment worth repeating until it bears the fruit that the Johannine Jesus would expect. I allude to the effort of early Christians to transform or leaven the imperial society by means of *two powerful symbolic gestures, sacraments of social transformation*, acted out with a persistent regularity. They are the weekly celebrations of the *Christian Sabbath* and the *Covenant Meal.*

I. Ever faithful to the ancient covenant of Israel, the early Christians turned Sunday into their Sabbath. It was as much a HOLIDAY **from work** as a HOLY DAY **for divine worship**, combining worship with a general strike from all labour, even for slaves. Worship was rendered to the "God of Slaves" through Jesus, the "Slave of God" *('ebed YHWH)*, who, under the imperial law of Caesar *(sub Pontio Pilato)*, had succumbed to a cruel death penalty meted out only to the slaves, the lowest stratum *(humiliores)* of the empire. Jesus was celebrated as the hope of the slaves, those deemed to have been condemned to a life of dehumanizing indebtedness. This was a provocative message to a political system that thrived on slavery.

II. On such weekly holidays, these Christians indulged in another similar act of silent protest against slavery, the economic base of the empire. While the Romans were kneeling before an altar in the temple where a leisure class of priests offered sacrificial victims to the gods of the powerful, the gods whose "mediator with humans" *(Pontifex Maximus)* was the emperor himself, the followers of Jesus did the exact opposite:- masters and slaves, males and females, Jews and Gentiles sat round a table in their homes as a community of equals, not only sharing the life of their God at a covenant meal but also exercising their royal and priestly co-victimhood in, with, and through Christ. The table challenged the altar; the meal defied the cult; the home dwarfed the temple; the fellowship of equals questioned the pyramid of power; a priestly people sitting around with their God as their guest, host and food confronted gentile priests praying to idols with their back to the people who were kneeling in fear; the solidarity with the co-victims of Christ expressed in self-sacrifice undermined the cultic priesthood of the leisure class placating gods with ritual oblations; and finally, the God who had pitched Her tent among the slaves belied the gods invented by a slave-owning empire.

These two simple acts performed week after week were the gentle but consistently regular strokes of a hammer that, with time, could have crumbled an empire thriving on slavery. They were like David's sling, capable of pelting down a gigantic power. This was the only way, Christ's own way, of converting people from the attractions of the Roman empire, namely, the constant and consistent witnessing to a contrasting model of society where life and worship, with no show of pomp and power, anticipated the new age promised to humankind. Such *ecclesiolae,* or what we could call "little flocks of Christ" (or anachronistically, 'basic ecclesial communities'), proliferating in the empire, seemed to have been invested with the holiness of Christ as long as they retained their identity as the little ones *(microi).* To these our God revealed all things; She remained ever at home among the lowly ones *(tapeinoi),* with whom Christ identified himself. For holiness has been recognized as a distinguishing mark of the true church from ancient times and is derived from the church being poor and being with the poor.[143]

It follows, then, that the reclaiming of our original charisma —that is, our Christian uniqueness— is the task of the poor

---

[143] As to how this "mark of holiness" is derived from the church's option for the poor, see Jurgen Moltmann, *Church in the Power of the Holy Spirit* (London: SCM Press, 1977), pp. 352-55, Aloysius Pieris, "Ecumenism in the Churches and the Unfinished Agenda of the Holy Spirit," *Spiritus* 3 (Spring 2003): pp. 54-56, 65.

and the powerless, who have God as their covenant partner in the mission of redemption. We are here dealing with the essence of biblical Christianity, namely God's covenant with Egypt's slaves at Sinai in the First Testament, which was upheld, confirmed, and sealed anew by Jesus on Calvary, where he revealed himself as God's New Covenant with the victims of Mammon-worshippers. Jesus' scandalous predilection for the despised, which seemed exaggerated in the eyes of the privileged class,[144] was the way he lived out his unique mission of uniting, in his own person, God and the poor to form one covenanted salvific reality. In Jesus, therefore, both partners of this covenant, YHWH and the slaves of all times, can be encountered. Hence any community that claims to believe in Christ would show signs of allegiance to both signatories of the covenant: God and the poor. Association with the lowly ones, recommended by Paul to his more privileged Christians (Rom. 16:20), is the surest way to be associated with God in Jesus. The option to struggle with the poor is the *distinguishing* mark of the church's divine origin.

(II) Recovery of Christian Identity in (South) Asia Today

1. Liberation Theology

A recovery of our identity through a realigning of the church with God's poor was certainly in the air in various parts of the church and began to assume concrete expression in the 1970s. A movement for Christian socialism that assimilated the social doctrine and praxis of other religions had already been launched in Sri Lanka in the 1950s with the formation of the Christian Workers' Fellowship only a few years before the emergence of the Latin American counterpart. It seemed

---

[144]   W.G. Kummel, *Introduction to the New Testament, rev. ed.* (London: SCM Press, 1975), p. 139

that the Spirit was blowing particularly, though not exclusively, in the most non-Christian continent (Asia), as well as in the most Christian continent (South America). Certain theologians were beginning to reach out to YHWH's suffering servants in India (the *Dalits*) and Korea (the *Minjung*) as their mentors and partners in the task of restoring to the church its lost identity. And Christian identity seekers in Asia (where they constituted a minority among the Christian minority) were beginning to hear about the small efforts of small people in Latin America to accomplish the same task there. The news of the rise of basic ecclesial communities (reminiscent of the above mentioned *ecclesiolae* in the Roman Empire) in South America, where so many poor people and so many Christians were concentrated,[145] accompanied by the publication in 1971 of Gustavo Gutierrez's *Theology of Liberation,* fuelled the enthusiasm of Asian Christians who had already begun a similar journey.[146] Some Asian Christians who were skeptical about their own colleagues' involvement in this enterprise were awakened from their dogmatic slumber by Gutierrez's epoch-making thesis.

This was the most creative phase of theological thinking in our continent in recent times. Whatever novel and noble that we possess today can be traced back to those years. For the age-old missionary enthusiasm for preaching Christianity and making converts had by then reached an all-time low except in tribal areas. For there was an unsettling feeling that we Christians had lost our way. Some blamed Vatican II for this

---

[145]   M. de C. Azevedo, S.J., *The Basic Ecclesial Communities in Brazil: The Challenge of a New Way of Being the Church* (Washington, DC: Georgetown University Press, 1987), pp. 177-244
[146]   See the observations of Asians (Preman Niles and Tissa Balasuriya, both from Sri Lanka) at the International Ecumenical Congress of Theology, February 20 – March 2, Sao Paolo, Brazil, in *The Challenge of Basic Christian Communities,* ed. S. Torres and John Eagleson (Maryknoll, NY: Orbis Books, 1981), pp. 253-54 and 259-62.

crisis, whereas it was the vision of this council that pointed to the crisis and allowed us to find a way out. Anything good we had said and done seemed, at best, a duplication of whatever good had been said and done by other religionists. On the other hand, whatever looked new that distinguished us from them was, *in their eyes,* our organizational skills and material resources, which linked us with the colonial and neo-colonial powers. This association with and reliance on foreign sources of wealth and power seemed unique to Christianity, a sort of a "mark" of the church that allegedly revealed its Christian identity! This was also the critical diagnosis that had been made available to the church since the early nineteenth century by certain non-Christian reformers of South Asia such as Raja Ram Mohan Roy, Sir Syed Ahmed, Swami Vivekananda, and most of all Mahatma Gandhi —all of them admirers of Jesus and some of them even self-proclaimed "followers" of Jesus— who lamented that the church's concern for the poor was motivated not by the love of the poor in themselves but by the allegedly sinister goal of rescuing souls for the church from Hinduism, thus using the poor and their poverty as an alibi for foreign-financed proselytism.[147]

This harsh criticism took a new meaning in the 1970s when the aforementioned theologians began to realize that the church's lost identity could be regained only by an **"option for the poor"** *regarded as a mission in itself,* in contrast with the previous era's policy of an **"option for the church"** *motivating service to the poor.* There was a crucial demand for this paradigm shift, this new way of thinking about the

---

[147]   See M. V. Nadkarni, "Ethics and Relevance of Conversion: A Critical Assessment of Religious and   Social Dimensions in Gandhian Perspective," *Economic and Political Weekly* 38 (January 18-24, 2003): pp. 227-41. The author, however, exempts Mother Teresa from this accusation

Christian mission that was not easily understood by the church officials.[148]

2. New Missionary Policy for Recovering Christian Identity

The new missionary policy, that "the church is for the poor" rather than the other way around, promised a recovery of Christianity's lost identity. This policy consisted of a response to a twofold vocation, the struggle to be poor and the struggle for the poor. This double calling seemed to demand that *the poor be recognized as the true body of Christ rather than as potential converts to be added on to the ecclesial body.* The conflict between the church's claim to be Christ's body and Christ's claim that the poor are his body could be resolved only when the church becomes co-extensive with the "poor in Spirit" as well as the "poor by circumstances" who will judge the nations in the person of Christ, the end-time judge. It is these two categories of the poor that give the church its identity.

In the light of this new awareness, all·Christian attempts at *inculturation,* or the processes by which the church tried to wear *the cultural garb of other religions* without appropriating the liberative core of those same religions seemed in the eyes of a Buddhist observer, a camouflage used by beasts of prey.[149] Besides, the earliest instance of indigenization in Asia, which resulted in an apostolic community of Jesus-followers in Kerala (India) in the first century CE under the patronage of the Persian (East

---

[148] The Vatican's CDF (Congregation for Doctrine of Faith, then under Cardinal Seper), exchanged letters with my provincial expressing concern about my paper "Towards an Asian Theology of Liberation," read at this Asian Theological Consultation of the Ecumenical Association of Third World Theologians in 1979. This paper has been published in Aloysius Pieris, *An Asian Theology of Liberation* , Maryknoll, NY: Orbis Books, 1988), pp. 69-86

[149] G. Vithanage, "The New Look with a Note: A Comment on Fr. Mervyn Fernando's Article on 'Is Adaptation Outmoded?'" *Quest* (Colombo) 4 (1969): pp. 80-81

Syrian/Nestorian) Church, had unfortunately assimilated what was and still is a regrettable weakness of the Hindu *Culture*, namely the religiously justified practice of caste discrimination. It took a millennium and a half before the victims of this nefarious caste system could receive baptism at the hands of a Francis Xavier, though the species of Christianity that brought about this salutary change remained *culturally European*! Later efforts to indigenize this same Christianity (first in the sixteenth century by De Nobili and then in the nineteenth century by Gnostic Christians) are seen by Dalit theologians as a mere replacement of the European theology of domination with a Brahmanic theology of the same kind. Thus the so-called "crisis of mission" experienced in the 1970s was a misnomer for the long-overdue abandonment of that paradigm of evangelization, which those who employ the inculturation-liberation paradigm have rightly condemned as "inculturation without liberation".

Here, then, is the dilemma of the seekers of a Christian identity in South Asia:- What kind of witness *(martyrion)* would guarantee that the proclamation *(kerygma)* of the good news *(euangelion)* to the poor would inspire the conversion *(metanoia)* of both the oppressor and the oppressed, the rich and the poor, the elite and the marginalized, in such a way that the victims of injustice would be neither proselytized into the church nor abandoned to the sinful structures associated with the non-liberative socio-religious traditions? The resolution of this dilemma became possible as various political theologies of liberation began to emerge during the critical decades mentioned above[150] and, concomitantly, as the contours of a *liberational theology of religions*, inspired by the religiousness of poor, became better defined.

---

[150] See Aloysius Pieris, "Political Theologies of Asia," in *Blackwell Companion to Political Theology*, ed. Peter Scott and William T. Cavanaugh (Oxford: Blackwell, 2004) pp. 256-70

(III) Doing Theology of Religions as If the Poor Mattered

1. An Asian Perspective on the Vatican's Apprehensions

After issuing admonitions about Latin American liberation theology, the Congregation for the Doctrine of the Faith (CDF) and its president, Josef Ratzinger, began to show concern about Asian Christians and their theological approach to other religions. John Allen of the *National Catholic Reporter* has listed twelve such documents appearing within a span of twelve years (1989-2000), climaxing in *Dominus Jesus.*[151] The Christological content and the ecclesiological presuppositions of these documents, including certain misapprehensions of what the Asian theologians are actually saying,[152] provided the key to a correct understanding of the aforementioned paradigm shift, which Rome had failed to recognize and which some Asians may have failed to articulate.

Once Liberation Theology associated with Latin America had been dealt with, it was obvious that Asia's "inculturation theology" had to be called back to the twofold truth it had allegedly diluted: that Christ is the only universal agent of salvation and that the (Roman) Church is the absolutely essential channel of salvation. My surmise is that the CDF's non-Asian advisers in Rome and its Asian informants from our part of the world were unaware of the "inculturation-liberation debate" that polarized the Asian theologians in the late 1970s and early 1980s. For there is still a strand of inculturationist theology that has not assimilated the struggle *to be* poor and the struggle to be *with and for* the poor as

---

[151]   John L. Allen, "Perils of Pluralism, *"National Catholic Reporter,* September 15, 2000, www.natcath.com/NCR_Online/archives/091500e.htm (accessed August 10, 2006)
[152]   See Aloysius Pieris, "The Roman Catholic Perception of Other Religions and Other Churches after the Vatican's *Dominus Jesus,"* *East Asian Pastoral Review* 38 (2001): 1, pp. 207-30.

essential ingredients of authentic Christianity and has therefore ignored Christ's uniqueness and Christianity's identity.

It is common knowledge that some confusion arose around inculturation and liberation at the Asian Theological Consultation in 1979 —ironically, after my presentation of a paper in which I deliberately avoided the theme of inculturation, which was a non-issue for me; instead, I proposed a paradigm in which religiousness and poverty, each in its *liberating* as well as *enslaving* dimension, would serve as the two poles of a tension constituting the dynamics of an Asian theology of liberation. Later, some theologians read "religiousness" and "poverty" as their accustomed poles of inculturation and liberation, respectively, thus missing the new paradigm and its implications.[153]

The dust settled within a couple of years, and the Asian theologies of liberation, and they alone, moved forward along the binary track of religiousness and poverty with greater clarity. Their focus, in other words, was not on Asia's "cultures" as such but on the *liberative* dimension of their *religious core*; nor was their focus exclusively on the metacosmic religiosity of the so-called higher (scriptural) religions of Asia but equally on the localized cosmic religiosity of the poor. I introduced the use of the word *cosmic* to designate the "this-worldly religiosity" of the Asian poor, as contrasted with the "secular" viewpoint —that is, the "nonreligious this-worldliness" of Western liberals.[154] The term "cosmic, therefore, embraces the sacred worldliness of

[153] See Chapter III, Sections 6 & 7. For notes on this controversy, see Pieris, *Asian Theology of Liberation*, p. 88, p. 133 nn. 3 and 4.
[154] See my entry in Virginia Fabella and R.S. Sgirtharajah, eds., *Dictionary of the Third World* (Maryknoll, NY: Orbis Books, 2000), s.v. "cosmic/metacosmic religions" (where, regrettably, *this-worldly* has been misspelled *third-worldly*). See also Aloysius Pieris, *Fire and Water: Basic Issues in Asian Buddhism and Christianity* (Maryknoll, NY: Orbis Books, 1996), pp. 15-26.

tribal and clan cultures as well as popular interpretations and practices of scriptural religions at their grassroots level in Asian societies. As the history of Asia's various revolutionary struggles has amply demonstrated, the cosmic religiosity of the poor conceals an explosive potential for socio-spiritual liberation.[155] The Dalit, Minjung, and feminist theologies of Asia, all categorized under the rubric of liberation, definitely lean toward the cosmic.

Thus every effort at inculturation in Asia that tended to assimilate only the metacosmic religiosity of the elite without integrating the cosmic spirituality of the poor seemed to have ignored what ultimately spells out Christ's uniqueness as well as Christianity's identity. Furthermore, such attempts seemed to many of us nothing more than a mere duplication in Asia of what had regrettably happened in Europe since the Hellenization of Christianity. Both the Asian inculturationists and the Western Patriarchate's *defensores fidei* (defenders of the faith) who are censoring the former, actually think along the same shaky theological lines!! In other words, the traditional Western theology that serves as the norm of orthodoxy is no different from any Asian theology that does not have the struggle of the poor in its agenda, for they all have begun as a process of inculturation minus liberation and therefore harbour a Christology without a soteriology. They have failed to articulate the uniqueness of Christ and consequently the true identity of Christianity.

Christianity's *caesura*, (Karl Rahner's preferred term for the "neat break") from the cultural constraints of the Jewish cultural tradition, thanks to the decision of the apostles at the so-called Council of Jerusalem (Acts 15: 1-20), prevented the Jesus community from remaining a mere sect of Judaism and perhaps disappear as did the Essenes. Perhaps this was

---

[155]   Pieris, *Asian Theology of Liberation,* esp. pp. 98-108.

essential at the time, and it guaranteed Christianity's inculturation among non-Jews. The result was that the new religion took root among the cosmopolitan and even racially hybrid communities of Greek-educated Jews and Gentiles living in the urban centers of the Roman Empire.[156] Christianity was thus released from the Semitic culture only to be buried in a Hellenistic one. More significantly, the Christianity of the relatively poor class of people in Palestine, for whom Paul organized financial assistance from the richer Greek-speaking churches, evolved into a sophisticated brand of doctrinaire religiosity elaborated by the social elite. Paul's failure to communicate the core of Christian soteriology, the death and the resurrection of Jesus, to the sophisticated Greeks of Athens in their own philosophical idiom (Acts 17:16-34) and the lesson Luke tried to teach the nascent church by narrating it (or creating it?) seemed to have been forgotten by this time.[157]

This is most evident from Aloys Grillmeier's analysis of the way Christological controversies cropped up in the context of what he calls "pagan philosophy" and even more the way they were finally resolved by a resort to dogmatic formulas that smacked of Greek "metaphysics".[158] Elaborate speculations about the Incarnation replaced the main soteriological theme of the Christ-event. The fact that Nestorius's early Christology tended to be more soteriological, while his later work *Liber Heraclidis*, which was so orthodox as to approximate the future Chalcedonian definitions, was more ontological,[159] surely indicates that as we move further away from the Semitic idiom of the Bible

---

[156] Brown, *Introduction to the New Testament*, pp. 63-64
[157] According to current scholarly opinion, Luke's story is not historical; rather, it reflects his desire to show that Athens, the center of Hellenism, was also evangelized (Cwiekowski, *Beginnings of the Church*, p. 103)
[158] Aloys Grillmeier, *Christ in Christian Tradition*, vol. 1, *From the Apostolic Age to Chalcedon* (AD 451) (London: Mowbrays, 1975), pp. 36-37
[159] Ibid., p. 44

toward the Hellenistic ethos of the first councils the theological language becomes less soteriological and more ontological. The thoroughly European idiom of these councils, *pace* (with due deference to) Norman Tanner,[160] failed, unfortunately, to conserve the biblical doctrine of salvation.[161] Grillmeier, the authority on this matter, has complained that, in the traditional Christology emanating from these first councils, "a development was at hand which is still a burden to Christology, the divorce between the person and the work of Jesus, between Christology and soteriology."[162]

Thus the "inculturation" of Christianity in the elitist culture of the Hellenistic world resulted in an eclipse of soteriology: it neglected the message of 'liberation' proclaimed through the life, work, death, and resurrection of Jesus. This traditional Christology missed what constitutes the uniqueness of Christ. The **God-man concept** lying behind the doctrine of the *Incarnation* eclipsed the **God-poor covenant** sealed on the *Cross*. The theology that the CDF employs as the norm of orthodoxy, derived from this same Christology, on the one hand, and the theology that the same CDF has censored in Asia, on the other, have both failed to address the question of Christ's uniqueness and Christianity's identity. The reason is that they both originated as a process of inculturation that did not take into account the liberation of the oppressed and oppressors. Therefore, any Asian theology of religion that is dictated by the poor not only is innocent of

---

[160] Norman Tanner, *Is the Church Too Asian? Reflections on the Ecumenical Council* (Bangalore: Dharmaram Publications, 2002).
[161] As I have argued in my review of Tanner's thesis in *Vidyajyoti: Journal of Theological Reflection* 67 (September 2003): pp. 782-92, and in the ensuing discussion between us: his response in *Vidyajyoti* 67 (November 2003): pp. 948-54; my reflection on his response in *Vidyajyoti* 68 (April 2004): p. 301; his counter-reply in *Vidyajyoti* 68 (April 2004): pp. 302-4; and my concluding comment in *Vidyajyoti* 68 (September 2004): pp. 702-3
[162] Aloys Grillmeier, *Christ in Christian Tradition*, vol. 2, *From the Council of Chalcedon to Gregory the Great* (590-604) (London: Mowbrays, 1987), pt. 1, p. 5.

the CDF's charge of diluting the uniqueness of Christ but throws that accusation back on the Roman censors themselves.

To sum up: both the CDF and the Asian theologies of inculturation which the CDF criticizes are unconscious advocates of "inculturation without liberation". What we uphold here cannot fall under either of these categories as we have set aside the inculturation-liberation paradigm as a misleading framework for theologizing in Asia. Ratzinger's claim that the Hellenistic framework of the traditional theology of the Western Patriarchate is *normative* for Christianity [even in Asia] implies that the inculturation of the Gospel message in the Greco-Roman philosophical tradition, which neglected soteriology or liberation in its basic dogmas (as observed by Grillmeyer), determines Catholic orthodoxy even for us! No wonder that in *Deus Caritas Est,* the same author, while discussing the "God of the Old Testament" observes a deafening silence about the *Exodus* (liberation) but goes out of the way to mention Aristotle, the Greek Thinker! Asia's *liberation* theologies have not come under the CDF's scrutiny but are, nevertheless, a virulent critique of both the CDF's theology and the theology it repudiates for replacing Hellenist thought with Indic philosophy and practices!

2. The Option for the Poor and the Asian Method of Doing Theology

Asian theologies of religion that are dictated by the poor show a two-pronged methodology. First, they seek a fresh understanding of the Scriptures in their Semitic/Asian idiom in order to prevent the justice dimension of biblical faith from being drowned in philosophical speculations, Asian or Greek. Second, they vernacularize theological education in the context of Asia's poverty, with a concomitant assimilation of the soteriological thrust of Asian cultures.[163]

The first strategy imposes on us a long-overdue *caesura* or rupture from the European particularity of the church's traditional theology so that we may re-read the biblical message of liberation in its Asian/Semitic idiom, unhampered by the Hellenism of the Christological councils, while adhering to the content of their dogmas. This is an extended version of the strong plea made by the late Stanislaus Lyonnet, S.J., that when we read the Bible, even the Septuagint and the New Testament, which are in Greek, "we must not have recourse to the (thought patterns of the) Greeks" (*non dobbiamo recorrere ai Greci)*, lest we grossly misinterpret the message of revelation, as has happened so often in traditional theology.[164]

We are convinced that the Chalcedonian Christology, circumscribed as it is in the philosophical language of the Greeks, not only presents a rather diminished figure of Christ compared to that of the scriptural Christ but also poses a serious obstacle to our proclamation of Christ in Asia because it either makes no sense at all when transposed into certain Asian languages assuming that a translation is possible,[165] or makes him one of the many incarnations *(avatars)* of god-men in the Hindu tradition,[166] or, as in a Buddhist context, reduces Christ to one of the many non-

---

[163]   The Sāvanā (Asian Institute of Missiology), directed by the Scripture scholar Dr. Shirley Lal Wijeysingha and the ecclesiologist Rev. Dr. Hilarion Dissanayaka, O.M.I., in Sri Lanka, follows this methodology, as do a few of the Jesuit Regional Theologates in India.

[164]   Stanislao Lyonnet, *Il Nuovo Testamento alla luce dell'Antico,* Studi Biblici Pastorali 3 (1968; reprint, Brescia: Paideia, 1972), pp. 36-37

[165]   I am supported in this by J. Neuner, S.J., "Mission Theology after Vatican II", *Vidyajyoti: Journal of Theological Reflection* 58 (April 1994): p. 213

[166]   For a thorough discussion of this topic, see J. Neuner, "Das Christus-Mysterium und die indische Lehre von den Avataras," in *Das Konsil von Chalcedon und Gegenwart* (Wuerzburg: Echter, 1954), pp. 786-824

transcendent and non-salvific cosmic forces *(devas)*, contrary to the intentions of Chalcedon.[167] Asian theologians can fall into this same rut if they too are tempted to speculate about Christ in terms of the many Asian philosophies that have been manufactured by the leisure class instead of trying to recapture the biblical message of liberation in the context of the soteriological aspirations of Asia's religious poor.

This is what has made me plead for a Covenant Christology, according to which Jesus, as the crucified, risen Christ or the life-giving Spirit, is the new covenant between God and the powerless, or the new law of love. In proposing this approach, I have responded to an ancient Asian (Judaic) impulse that Grillmeier himself mentions in passing: the identification of Jesus as the covenant *(diatheke)* and as the law *(nomos)*.[168] With this approach, we could spell out what Chalcedon's God-man concept had failed to articulate, namely, the uniqueness of Christ, neither under-estimating the soteriological role of other religions nor ignoring, as Chalcedon was doing, the clamour of God's poor for justice and freedom.[169] Since I have elaborated this vision in the many sources quoted above, all I shall do here is to articulate a few aspects of it.

In the first place, the justice dimension of the biblical faith, mentioned above as the first prong of our strategy, requires a clarification because, ever since the Roman Synod of 1971, the inseparable link between the preaching of the Gospel and the liberation of the poor has been expressed as a combination of "[the proclamation of] faith and [the promotion of] justice" in an explicitly anti-biblical sense. The confusion originated from our traditional theology,

---

[167]   Aloysius Pieris, "Christologies in Asia: A Reply to Felipe Gomez," *Voices from the Third World* 11 (1989): pp. 155-72
[168]   Grillmeier, *Christ in Christian Tradition*, 1: p. 44
[169]   Aloysius Pieris, "Christ beyond Dogma: Doing Christology in the Context of the Religions and the Poor," *Louvain Studies* 25 (2000): pp. 187-231

where justice is a merely human virtue, which therefore is not salvific unless informed by the infused theological virtue of faith. Here the Chalcedonian mentality, which is patently operative, is compounded by a Roman juridical notion of justice[170] No wonder that a complaint was persistently heard in the post-synodal era that the struggle for justice, understood in this scholastic sense, had eclipsed the faith dimension of our mission. This confusion seems to have compelled John Paul II to issue the encyclical *Dives in misercordia* to show how God mitigates justice with forgiving love and saving mercy.

Let us therefore, turn once more to Lyonnet. Contrary to the current theological understanding of justice, he insists, the biblical notion of justice is not to be confused with the end-time judgment (condemnation) of the unjust, for which the appropriate biblical term is God's wrath *(orge tou theou);* therefore, the biblical notion of justice does not need to be mitigated by God's redeeming and forgiving love, as presupposed in the current theological parlance. Rather, justice in the Bible is always an expression of God's mercy and love, which forgives and saves rather than judges and condemns. It is none other than God's own fidelity to the covenant,[171] that is, God's partiality to the powerless who are God's covenant partners, summoning the oppressors to repentance and conversion. Even the end-time judgment, God's wrath, can be avoided by partaking in God's justice to the poor. We are dealing with the covenant spirituality in which God's love is extended both to sinners and to those who are sinned against, a spirituality that must pervade the church's entire lifestyle, liturgy, and pastorate.

---

[170] As substantiated in Pieris, *God's Reign for God's Poor,* pp. 19-24 and esp. pp. 48-51
[171] Lyonnet, *Il Nuovo Testamento,* 49ff, esp. 61-64

This spirituality, therefore, is our faith-response to that covenant, our participation in the justice of the covenant. Our faith is not merely **our trust in God** whose justice never fails the little ones who are his covenant partners but also our own unfailing fidelity to that same covenant — that is, **our solidarity with the poor.** What is even more significant, the Just One's end-time judgment or "wrath" *(orgē)* is passed by the little ones of today who are covenanted with him (Matt. 25:36ff.). Therefore our **faith** expresses the covenantal **justice** to the oppressed in view of the eschatological judgment that the victim-judge of nations would pass on the oppressors who fail to repent and cooperate with that same divine justice. Our faith, therefore, impels us to seek the conversion of the unjust.

Since the justice dimension of biblical faith is thus traced back to the covenant between God and the poor —a covenant enfleshed as Jesus the Christ— every kind of God-talk (theology) must invariably revolve around the poor: It must be a Christology in which the Asian poor as well as the Asian religions are taken in their dialectical relationship, as befits the soteriological thrust of Asian cultures. This means that Christ, in whom "the God of the violated" is also "the violated God" prophesied in the servant songs of Isaiah and thematized in the Passion narratives of the Gospels, can only be good news, and never a threat either to the Asian poor or to the Asian religions, their founders or their adherents.

3. God's Reign for God's Poor
When Jesus refers to the poor as part of God's realm of the saved, he does so without attaching any religious label to them. Blessed are the poor, not because they are potential converts to the church but because they are poor. Not only the poor in spirit (Matt. 5:3), or the "detached ones" associated with Asia's metacosmic religiosity, but also the socially poor (Luke 6:20) and the "dispossessed ones" with

211

their cosmic spirituality are the stuff that the reign of God is made of. The church, being the servant and sacrament of God's reign, is defined by its identification with these two categories of the poor, who therefore give Christianity its identity. Christ is one body with them already; they do not have to be converted to the church. For the radical conversion *(šûb, metanoia)* he demands as a condition for salvation is not a change of one's religion (or proselytism, which he ridiculed in Matt. 23:15) but a change of one's life —that is, the acceptance of the beatitudinal spirituality (greedless or non-idolatrous living), which happens to be the common soteriological thrust of all Asian cultures.

This means that God's enemies are not other religionists, as the fundamentalist Christians believe, but the Mammon-worshippers, of all religions and no religion, who create poverty. To them the church must dauntlessly proclaim from housetops and public places the need for conversion. This is true evangelism. Our mission to them is to demonstrate that God's wrathful judgment and God's merciful justice are both mediated by the poor themselves. For the Christ whom we believe in and proclaim to the world is not merely a divine person or a divine substance assuming human nature but a **corporate person** *in whom God is one body with the victims of human greed.* It is in terms of this Christology that we claim that the option for the poor constitutes *our service to Christ in the poor* whereas the administration of word and sacraments in the church represents *Christ's service to us through his ministers.* The former (traditionally misnamed "corporal works of mercy") is in the order of salvation, whereas the sanctification and fortification received in the Baptism and the Eucharist (known traditionally as "spiritual works of mercy") are in the second order as sacramental expressions of the salvific event that happens in the first order. Here again the liberation perspective forces us to turn upside down the traditional order in which service to the poor

212

(condition for salvation or final liberation according to Christ) is regarded as less important soteriologically than sacramental ministries!

If this is the Christological understanding of the sacraments, then surely Christ's mission mandate to baptize and make disciples of all nations is a command to continue his own mission, the mission for which he was anointed by the Spirit at Nazareth (Luke 4:17-21): to liberate the victims of oppression, the poor, the captives, those in pain of heart and body, and to declare the Jubilee year, which grants end-time amnesty to the oppressors so that they might be reconciled with their victims by submitting to the covenantal stipulations. It was to achieve this mission that Jesus received his own baptism on the cross (for this is what Jesus always meant by his baptism), in solidarity with his co-victims of all ages in the end-time of Calvary.

Those who impose this cross on the masses, then and now, are *idolaters*, and not necessarily *atheists*; among the latter one might often find promoters of justice. The baptism of a nation and its conversion to the discipleship of the beatitudes consists of a death-bringing struggle to break down the vicious idols that enslave that nation: religious bigotry, national pride, racial prejudice, class elitism, military superiority, gender discrimination, colour consciousness, and language domination. The social conflict (i.e., the "cross") that the church and the nation face in this anti-idolatrous mission is also their share in the saving baptism of Christ. A nation is baptized into Christ when it has become a community of equals with no trace of indiscrimination and injustice of any kind.

That this missiology meets strong and fierce resistance from fundamentalist groups both Catholic and otherwise here in

Asia is very well known.[172] In their view, Christ is involved in a conversion race with the founders of other religions rather than being persecuted in His members by the worshipers of the money demon. They have not identified the real enemy, the attractive beast which brands its worshipers with its ugly identity mark (Rev. 16:2; 19:20) and which can rob the church of its identity if the church does not live its option for the poor. They have not discovered that if we were as self-effacingly humble as our Master was, other religionists would join us as partners in a common mission, the mission of baptizing nations into beatitudinal living, as has happened in many parts of Asia in some visible measure through basic human communities. Nor do these Christian zealots believe that Christ's uniqueness is revealed only when he draws all hearts to himself from the cross (John 12:32-33), where he is being baptized, and that our own identity as Christians lies precisely in following that ideal rather than in elating our collective ego by advertising a mass-mesmerizing Messiah. The basic human communities acting like leaven in human society on the one hand and the colourful mass rallies of some triumphalistic Christian sects on the other hand witness to two conflicting images of Christ and Christianity in Asia today.

Roman as well as non-Roman evangelicals have expressed their strong reservations with regard to our missionary

---

[172] A few random examples: in Sri Lanka a Catholic bishop tried hard to use the resources of the heavily funded "Holy Childhood" to disestablish the inter-religious and locally self-reliant children's movement called *lakrivi,* spread across the country by the Oblates of Mary Immaculate, who had subscribed to the new missiology. Evangelistic pastors from Korea who were influenced by the U.S. based fundamentalist sects (which undermined the struggles of Minjung Christians and Minjung theologians) opened missions in Sri Lanka polarizing a particular denomination that had, till recently, many advocates of the new missiology even among its leadership. Other evangelists, financially backed by rich Christian organizations in the West, have infuriated the Buddhists by their fanatical acts of breaking Buddha statues and burning sacred objects as part of their policy of proselytism, interpreting the Buddhist reaction to their insensitivity as persecution. This is a repetition of what Portuguese missionaries did in the sixteenth century.

approach. "How can your understanding of baptism and discipleship of nations be reconciled with the mass conversions to the church that the apostles encouraged immediately after Pentecost under the impulse of the Holy Spirit (Acts 2)?" In response to this objection, we draw their attention to what the Spirit is saying to the churches today and how we ought to respond to that Word by following another precedent recorded in the same book of the Acts.

First, the situation of the Mediterranean region during the time of Acts 2 radically differs from what we experience in South Asia today. In the post-Pentecostal decades, the religion of the Romans and the Greeks was on the wane and there was a spiritual vacuum that, providentially, served as the entry point for Christ's message of liberation into what was then supposed to be the civilized world. Our situation here in South Asia is quite the opposite. It is precisely that same Christianity which is now in crisis, while, on the contrary, the non-Christian religions are not on the decline but very much self-assertive and capable of inculcating anti-idolatrous beatitudinal spirituality, notwithstanding the persistence of many negative elements that are not absent in Christianity either. Our own solidarity with them in the anti-idolatrous spirituality common to all religions can ensure our own renewal as well as their perseverance in the path of covenantal justice.

Moreover, and more significantly, the five-hundred-year-old failure of Christianity to effect mass conversions in this part of the globe, in contrast with its almost total success in Latin America, the Philippines, and Oceania, is a phenomenon that must serve as a sign of the time revealing what the Spirit is saying to the churches in South Asia.[173] To read God's design

---

[173] For a socio-historical analysis of this situation, see Aloysius Pieris, "Does Christ Have a Place in Asia," *Concilium* 2 (1993), pp. 33-47, reprinted as ch. 7 in Pieris, *Fire and Water*, pp. 65-78

215

through this remarkable datum of history, and also to act according to that reading, we could follow another precedent mentioned in Acts 15: the radically revolutionary decision to exempt the Gentiles from the divinely ordained initiation rite of Israel, something that parallels the ritual baptism in the church. By whose authority did the apostles change this sacrosanct obligation of **ritual circumcision** issuing from the revealed law of God?

It was indeed a synergistic decision made by the Spirit and the Apostles in the light of new evidence brought from the frontiers of the church (Antioch). The power of binding and loosing, which Israel's leaders claimed to have received from God, was, to use a later Jewish expression, the authority to determine *halakkah*, to decide what practices should be followed by the community,[174] rather than what new dogmas should be imposed on the believers. This very same authority of binding and loosing was given by Christ to his disciples, obviously as the power of discretion in the matter of making policy changes in the praxis of the church. The apostles, guided by the Spirit, exercised this authority under pressure from frontier ministers such as Paul and Barnabas in changing the pristine practice of ritual circumcision sanctioned by Scripture and the sacred tradition. So do the frontier ministers working in South Asia, today, press on the church to promulgate the **non-ritual** but more radical form of **baptism** and conversion to discipleship that our option for Christ and his co-victims has disclosed to us.[]

---

[174]   David H. Stern, introduction to *Jewish New Testament*, ed. David H. Stern (Jerusalem: Jewish New Testament Publications, 1994), p. xxiii

OTHER WORKS BY THE AUTHOR
Prepared by
Sr Frances de Silva RGS
(Archivist, Tulana)

(a) Books already published

1. *AN ASIAN THEOLOGY OF LIBERATION,* Orbis Books,
Maryknoll, NY 1988.
<u>German</u>: *Theologie der Befrieing in Asien:Christentum im Kontext
der Armut und Religionen,* Herder, Freiburg, 1986.
<u>French</u>: *Une theologie asiatique de la liberation,* Centurion
(Paris_ 1990.
<u>Italian</u> : *Una teologia asiatica della liberazione,* Cittadella, Assisi,
1990
<u>Korean</u> (from the German original which has more chapters than
the English one)
<u>Vietnamese</u> (from the English version)
(<u>Spanish</u> version mentioned under no.3 below differs from the
above and has been translated into French too,)

2. *LOVE MEETS WISDOM: A CHRISTIAN EXPERIENCE OF
BUDDHISM,* Orbis Books, Maryknoll, 1988.
<u>German</u> : *Liebe und Weisheit: Begegnung von Cristentum und
Buddhismus,* Grenewald, Mainz, 1989.

3. *EL ROSTRO ASIATICO DE CRISTO,* Verdad e Imagen,
Ediciones Sigueme, Salamanca, 1991;
<u>French</u> : *Le visage asiatique de Christ,* Edition de Cerf. Paris.

4. *FIRE AND WATER: BASIC ISSUES IN ASIAN BUDDHISM AND
CHRISTIANITY,* Maryknoll, Orbis Books, Maryknoll, 1996.
<u>German</u>: *Feuer und Wasser: Frau, Gesellschaft, Spiritualitaet in
Buddhismus und Christentum,* Herder, Freiburg, 1994.
<u>Spanish</u>: *Liberacion, inculturacion, dialogo religioso: un nuevo
paradigma desde Asia,* Editorial Verbo Divino, 2001.

5. *GOD'S REIGN FOR GOD'S POOR: A RETURN TO THE JESUS FORMULA*, Tulana Jubilee Publications, Kelaniya, 1999. Spanish version : *El Reino de Dios para los Pobres de Dios*, by *Ediciones Mensajero*, Bilbao (2005).

6. *MYSTICISM OF SERVICE* (A Short Course on Christian Spirituality) Tulana Publications, Kelaniya, 2000

7. *CHRISTHOOD OF JESUS AND THE DISCIPLESHIP OF MARY: AN ASIAN PERSPECTIVE*, Logos (39), CSR, Colombo, 2002.

8. *STUDIES IN THE PHILOSOPHY AND THE LITERATURE OF PALI ĀBHIDHAMMIKA BUDDHISM*, EISD 2004.

9. *NĀSARATAYĒ JESU HÀ BHĀRATAYE YESUS*, Sāvanā Publicatons, No. 8, CSR, Colombo 2005.

10. *PROPHETIC HUMOUR IN BUDDHISM AND CHRISTIANITY : DOING INTER-RELIGIOUS STUDIES IN THE REVERENTIAL MODE*, EISD, Colombo, 2005.
Portuguese: *Viver e Arriscar: Etudios Interreligiosos Comparativos a parti de Uma Perspectiva Asiatica*, Nhanduti Editoria, Sao Bernardo do Campo, 2008
Italian : *Umorismo profetico nel Buddhismo e Cristianiesimo: Strudi interreligiosi nella modalita del respecto*. A cura di don Antonio Lecce

11. *PSALMS, POEMS AND SONGS: THEOGRAPHICAL SKETCHES FROM A JESUIT'S DIARY (1974-2006)*, Tulana, Gonawala-Kelaniya , 2006

12. *GIVE VATICAN II A CHANCE: YES TO INCESSANT RENEWAL, NO TO REFORM OF THE REFORMS*, Kelaniya 2010

13. *OUR UNHIDDEN AGENDA: HOW WE JESUITS WORK PRAY AND FORM OUR MEN*, Tulana Research Centre, Kelaniya 2012.

14. *FR FRANK'S CONFESSIONS: SEVEN DAYS FROM HIS DIARY*, (Fiction) Centre for Society and Religion, Colombo, 2013.

15. *PROVIDENTIAL TIMELINESS OF VATICAN II: A LONG OVERDUE HALT TO A SCANDALOUS MILLENNIUM?* Tulana Media Unit, Kelaniya, Sri Lanka, 2013

16. *THE GENESIS OF AN ASIAN THEOLOGY OF LIBERATION: AN AUTOBIOGRAPHICAL EXCURSUS ON THE ART OF THEOLOGIZING IN ASIA,* Tulana Media Unit, Kelaniya, 2014

(c) Books to be published in the immediate future

17. *Mind and Matter in Buddhist Epistemology*

18. *Religious Life and Vows : Another Perspective*

19. *A Trilogy on Human Rights*

(d) Books *edited* by the author

1. Shri Charles de Silva, *Parama Puda* ("Supreme Sacrifice", a Passion Play), as a special issue of *Sankha* (1996) published by the Ministry of Culture (Sri Lanka Government).

2. Shri Charles de Silva, *Raja Upatha,* (Birth of a King), published by the Tulana Media Unit, Kelaniya, with music by the Sri Lankan Folk Musician, Rohana Baddage. (An audio-version with leading radio artists reading the texts with Music, and already presented as a radio play during Christmas).

3. S.G.Perera, s.j., *Historical Sketches,* Third Print, Godage Brothers, Colombo 2013.

(d) Journals *edited* by the author
1. *Dialogue New Series,* since 1974, published by the Ecumenical Institute, Colombo 6

2. *Vāgdevī, Journal of Religious Reflection* (New Series), since 2007, published by the Tulana Media Unit, Kelaniya.

3   Retired member of the Editorial Board of *Concilium*

· **(e) Articles published in local and international journals and in anthologies** : Over 250 articles in European languages are preserved in the archives of Tulana and available for reference. These articles deal with theology (all aspects of it), Indology (Indic philosophies, religions, spiritualities, specifically Pali literature, Buddhist doctrine and practice) as well as Inter-religious dialogue and ecumenism. Those in Sinhala (not listed here) are also available for consultation.

(f) From citations in other articles, it is possible to conclude that about *fifty (50) post-graduate and other studies have been made on the theology of the author*. Only a few are available in the Tulana archives.

(g) Memberships
1. Pali Text Society, (PTS) Oxford;

2. Sri Lanka Association of Buddhist Studies (SLABS); honorary membership was offered by the SLAB in recognition of his contribution to Buddhist Research.

3. Advisory Board of *Dilatato Corde* (based in USA)

4. Board of Advisors to the Jesuit General on inter-religious dialogue and ecumenism. (2010-2012).

(h) Lectureships and Professorships
In 20 Universities in Europe, America and Asia. (names of universities and other details found in the Tulana archives.)

□□□□□□□□□□□